T0254148

Microsoft Mapping

Geospatial Development in Windows 10
with Bing Maps and C#

Second Edition

Carmen Au
Ray Rischpater

Apress®

Microsoft Mapping: Geospatial Development in Windows 10 with Bing Maps and C#

ISBN-13 (pbk): 978-1-4842-1444-2

ISBN-13 (electronic): 978-1-4842-1443-5

Managing Director: Welmoed Spahr
Lead Editor: James DeWolf
Development Editor: Douglas Pundick
Technical Reviewer: Fabio Claudio Ferrachiati
Editorial Board: Steve Anglin, Mark Beckner, Gary Cornell, Louise Corrigan, Jim DeWolf,
    Jonathan Gennick, Robert Hutchinson, Michelle Lowman, James Markham, Susan McDermott,
    Matthew Moodie, Jeffrey Pepper, Douglas Pundick, Ben Renow-Clarke, Gwenan Spearing,
    Matt Wade, Steve Weiss
Coordinating Editor: Melissa Maldonado
Copy Editor: April Rondeau
Compositor: SPi Global
Indexer: SPi Global
Artist: SPi Global

Distributed to the book trade worldwide by Springer Science+Business Media New York, 233 Spring Street, 6th Floor, New York, NY 10013. Phone 1-800-SPRINGER, fax (201) 348-4505, e-mail orders-ny@springer-sbm.com, or visit www.springer.com. Apress Media, LLC is a California LLC and the sole member (owner) is Springer Science + Business Media Finance Inc (SSBM Finance Inc). SSBM Finance Inc is a Delaware corporation.

For information on translations, please e-mail rights@apress.com, or visit www.apress.com.

Apress and friends of ED books may be purchased in bulk for academic, corporate, or promotional use. eBook versions and licenses are also available for most titles. For more information, reference our Special Bulk Sales–eBook Licensing web page at www.apress.com/bulk-sales.

Any source code or other supplementary materials referenced by the author in this text is available to readers at www.apress.com. For detailed information about how to locate your book's source code, go to www.apress.com/source-code/.

Contents at a Glance

Contents

About the Authors

Carmen Au is a software developer at Uber. Prior to that, she was at Microsoft working on mapping technology. Her work in map navigation has been published in journals and at various academic conferences, and has been patented and featured in *New Scientist* magazine and on the CBS News website. Carmen received her B.Eng, M.Eng, and Ph.D. in Computer Engineering at McGill University, with her doctoral work being in Computer Vision and Augmented Reality.

Ray Rischpater is an engineer and author with over twenty years of experience writing about and developing software for mobile and Internet platforms.

During this time, he has participated in the development of Internet technologies and custom applications for Microsoft Windows, Java ME, Qualcomm BREW, Apple iPhone, Google Android, Palm OS, Apple Newton, and Magic Cap. Presently, he's employed as a software engineering manager at Uber.

When not writing for or about mobile platforms, he enjoys doing amateur radio with the call sign KF6GPE, photography, and hiking with his family and friends in and around the San Lorenzo Valley in central California.

About the Technical Reviewer

Fabio Claudio Ferracchiati is a senior consultant and a senior analyst/developer using Microsoft technologies. He works at BluArancio SpA (`www.bluarancio.com`) as a senior analyst/developer and Microsoft Dynamics CRM specialist. He is a Microsoft Certified Solution Developer for .NET, a Microsoft Certified Application Developer for .NET, a Microsoft Certified Professional, and a prolific author and technical reviewer. Over the past ten years, he has written articles for international magazines and coauthored more than ten books on a variety of computer topics.

Acknowledgments

We'd both like to thank all those at Apress involved in getting the second edition of this book to print, including our technical reviewer, Fabio, April Rondeau, and especially Melissa Maldonado for shepherding the project to conclusion. Also, a warm thanks to James DeWolf for asking us if anything had changed in the Microsoft mapping world with the release of Windows 10, giving us the opportunity to tell you about those changes.

We must also thank our teammates at Microsoft and Uber: while this was a personal project of ours done on our own time, our peers gave us the encouragement to work on the project, as well as opportunities to learn what we're showing you in this book and show them what we learned in writing this book for you.

Finally, we must thank our families for their patience as we spent time with our computers instead of them on those weekends and evenings that were our chance to bring this book to you.

Introduction

Mapping is at the heart of many of today's applications, from consumer web properties—such as review, real estate, and transportation sites—to mobile applications ranging from fitness applications to social networking applications. It's a broad discipline that includes databases (where you store spatial data), computation (how you process and organize the data), and visualization (how you place that information in front of the user). This book aims to give you a succinct introduction to all of these topics, showing you how to build location-aware applications on top of the tools that Microsoft provides.

Microsoft is not a newcomer to mapping, having entered the arena in 1997 with its Microsoft TerraServer website, which showed satellite and aerial imagery of the United States as an example of the scalability of Microsoft SQL Server and Windows NT. Since then, it has materially participated in developing software and solutions for mapping, including the addition of support for geospatial processing to Microsoft SQL Server; the creation of map controls for Windows and the web so as to render map data; the significant collection of geospatial data to support its Bing and Windows 10 properties; and the inclusion of geospatial processing in its support for SQL on Azure, Microsoft's cloud-computing platform

Who Is This Book For?

If you're developing an application that involves location, mapping, or geospatial processing and you're interested in using state-of-the-art platforms and tools in your application, this book is for you.

We assume you have some high-level familiarity with programming and computer science, but that you're not an expert in working with geospatial data. For many developers, your requirements may be as simple as "show a map," or "store every user's location." You need to know enough about mapping concepts—such as coordinate systems and services work—to design working systems, but you don't need to get down into the gritty details of how imagery is tiled spatially, or which routing algorithm the routing service uses. In this book, we aim for that middle road: give you enough information to build your application and understand the services you're using so that you can make appropriate design decisions as you work toward your goals.

We assume you have some familiarity with software development using C# and .NET. If you've never written a Windows application before, some of the chapters may be a little tough going, especially the chapters that discuss the use of the various Bing Maps controls for Windows Presentation Foundation and Windows 10. There are plenty of good resources on Windows development just a Bing or Google search away if you're coming to Windows for the first time.

What You'll Learn by Reading This Book

We want you to be as productive as possible with Microsoft's mapping offerings as quickly as possible. After reading this book, you will be able to do the following:

- Understand basic concepts about location-based programming, including the notion of coordinate systems, datums, geocoding, and reverse-geocoding

- Use the Bing Maps controls for the web and Windows to show map data in your applications

- Understand how you can use Microsoft SQL Server and SQL on Azure to store geospatial data

- Understand how you can use Microsoft Azure to host your web applications and services that power your web and mobile applications

- Know how to use the Bing Maps Services to obtain routes, latitude and longitude for addresses, and addresses for latitude and longitude, as well as to map tiles

- Know when using a tool like Power Map for Excel is better than writing your own map application for data visualization

The book's chapters are organized on specific themes. You should begin by reading Chapter 1, which introduces the basic concepts you need to know to build applications that use map data. There are important fundamentals there, so even if another chapter has caught your eye, be sure to at least skim it. In that chapter, we also provide an outline of the rest of the book so that you can decide what to read next. If you're in a hurry to build a back end for your application, continue to the next few chapters to read about Microsoft Azure and SQL on Azure; if you're interested in using a specific map control, skip ahead to the chapter about that particular map control.

In nearly every chapter, we've taken a tutorial step-by-step approach showing you how to replicate our results. It's important that you follow along, especially if you're new to the Microsoft way of doing things, in order to get the most out of what we're offering. Most of the chapters also have a significant body of code for you to use as a starting point for your own work.

Enough preliminaries—it's time to turn the page and dig into exactly how to make the most of Microsoft's mapping services!

CHAPTER 1

Getting Started with Microsoft and Mapping

Location and mapping play an increasingly important role in software today. The advent of location-aware social applications; websites like Bing Maps, Google Maps, and Yelp; mobile mapping and navigation applications; and location-aware games like Shadow Cities by Grey Area have all increased customer demand for software that knows, presents, and uses your location in helpful ways.

Building these applications from scratch is not easy; in addition to the usual issues of scaling and software development in general, location-aware applications pose additional problems in the areas of content (such as the underlying map, points of interest, traffic, and routing) and the back-end storage necessary to quickly index, store, and search data by its position on the Earth. Open-source solutions exist; many database vendors have SQL extensions for storing data such as latitude and longitude, and there are user-interface controls for a number of platforms, such as Google Maps for the web and controls on Android and iOS. Only Microsoft, however, provides a soup-to-nuts solution for writing location-aware applications, including

- Microsoft SQL Server, which provides support for geospatial types and operations;

- SQL Database, Microsoft's Azure-hosted SQL Server solution;

- Windows Azure, which provides platform-as-a-service (PaaS) and infrastructure-as-a-service (IaaS) solutions for hosting your application's services;

- Bing Maps controls for presenting maps with your data on the web and in native applications on Windows; and

- services provided for traffic and routing overlaid on Bing Maps controls.

After reading this chapter, you'll have a good understanding of how Microsoft technologies can help you build your location-aware application, how this book is organized, and where to turn next to learn the gritty details you need to build your application.

Mapping and Microsoft

Microsoft has a long history in providing software for mapping, starting with Microsoft MapPoint (first launched in 2000) and TerraServer, a collaboration between Microsoft Research (MSR) and the United States Geological Service (USGS) in continuous operation from 1998 through May of 2012, as well as the various iterations of web-based mapping solutions culminating in Bing Maps. In addition to making map data available in commercial software and online, Microsoft also makes its map control available for Windows, permitting native-application developers access to the same visual presentation as Microsoft provides on its websites. In addition, Microsoft has provided significant back-end support for applications that use location and map data, starting with support for geospatial data types that was introduced in Microsoft SQL Server 2008 and continues in releases through the present day. More recently, Microsoft has made these features of Microsoft SQL Server available as part of the SQL Database service on Windows Azure, Microsoft's cloud computing service. Let's take a closer look at the capabilities Microsoft provides.

Bing Maps for Developers

You may already be familiar with Bing Maps on the web, especially if you use Bing when you search for points of interest like restaurants and businesses. Although not as widely adopted in mash-ups and other applications as Google Maps is, Bing Maps has a developer API comparable with Google Maps, letting you develop asynchronous JavaScript and XML (AJAX) applications for the web. This AJAX API lets web developers build map-aware applications that can

- display street and aerial maps of any region, letting the user zoom and pan the map presented;

- annotate a displayed map with markers, lines, and regions organized in overlays, letting you add your data to the map;

- plot directions and traffic information provided by Bing Maps;

- obtain indoor venue maps for many shopping districts and indoor venues;

- geocode (determine the latitude and longitude for an address) and reverse geocode (determine an address for a latitude and longitude) to refine your user experience; and

- Search for businesses using Bing.

In addition to making a web control available, Microsoft makes an embeddable map control available with similar features. This map control, which you can see in Figure 1-1, supports most of the same features as the AJAX version and is available for Windows 10 (for Windows Universal Applications), as well as for Windows Presentation Foundation (WPF). There are also older controls for Windows 8, Windows Phone, and Apple iOS.

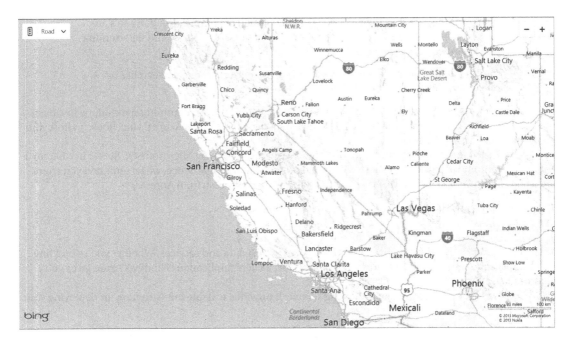

Figure 1-1. *A native Bing Maps control*

The new native control part of Windows 10 has some new features, too, including a beautiful 3D aerial mode with camera control and integration with Microsoft's Streetside, giving you on-the-ground imagery of buildings and storefronts that is rapidly growing in coverage to include the entire United States.

Learning how to use the various flavors of the Bing Maps control is a key part of this book, and we will spend a lot of time discussing the various features available to you and the versions that exist. For more information about the control, see Chapters 5 and 6 (where we discuss the web version of the control), Chapter 7 (where we discuss the WPF version of the control), and Chapter 8 (where we discuss the Windows 10 version of the control).

Microsoft SQL Server for Location Applications

A growing number of databases support extensions for geospatial applications, and Microsoft SQL Server is no exception. In Microsoft SQL Server 2008, Microsoft introduced data types for both round-Earth and planar (projective) mapping. In addition to data types for storing geospatial data, Microsoft added support for Simple Feature Access (ISO 19125) and support for two-dimensional geographic data, including about seventy methods from the specification. In 2012, with Microsoft SQL Server 2012, Microsoft significantly extended this support, adding new methods and new types of geometry for specific applications.

With its spatial extensions in Microsoft SQL Server, you can

- store points, lines, polygons, and other shapes in a flat coordinate system using the geometry spatial data type;

- store points, lines, polygons, and other shapes in a round-Earth coordinate system using the geography data type;

- perform computations on collections of points, such as computing a polygon's area or perimeter, determining if a point falls inside or outside a region, and determining the intersection between regions; and

- build spatial indices over spatial data, letting you perform database searches by location quickly over thousands or millions of points.

You can access Microsoft SQL Server's location-based features if you're running stand-alone instances of Microsoft SQL Server, as well as in the SQL Database service on Windows Azure if you choose to host your application on Windows Azure.

We will provide a gentle introduction to storing geospatial data using Microsoft SQL Server in Chapter 3. For a more thorough treatment for those with professional database experience, we recommend you check out a copy of *Pro Spatial with SQL Server 2012* by Alistair Aitchison, also from Apress.

Windows Azure to Host Your Application

Most applications today require a back-end component to host data and services. Whether you're building a web application or just the back-end services to support a client application, Windows Azure gives you a platform on which to deploy your services.

Windows Azure is more than just a hosting service; it provides scalable infrastructure for deploying your services, including

- easy partitioning into storage, web, and worker hosts running Windows Server in one or more geographic regions for redundancy;

- relational storage through the SQL Database service;

- NoSQL table storage through key-value pairs, as well as the storage of blobs and smaller data blocks (ideal for inter-host communication and processing) through queues;

- inter-host messaging through the Windows Azure Service Bus; and

- support for Microsoft's web hosting through Microsoft Internet Information Services (IIS), letting you serve static as well as dynamic content through Active Server Pages (ASP) with ASP.NET and ASP Model-View-Controller (MVC) (or, if you prefer, PHP or Node.js).

In this book, we will discuss Windows Azure as it pertains to hosting location-aware applications in the cloud, especially as a host for running the SQL Database Service and Microsoft IIS. In Chapter 2, you'll get started with your own trial Azure account and deploy a simple Bing Maps application for the web. In Chapters 3 and 4 you will learn how to configure the SQL Database Service to store data for your application and construct Windows Communication Foundation (WCF) endpoints for your web and native client applications. If that's not enough about Windows Azure for you, we recommend *Windows Azure Platform* by Tejaswi Redkar and Tony Guidici, also from Apress.

Maps without Code: Microsoft Power Map

Sometimes you just need to visualize a data set on a map, either as part of developing a larger solution or just to examine a particular data set. While you can write custom data-visualization code using the Bing Maps control for the web or desktop, in many cases it's easier to load your data into Microsoft Excel and use Microsoft Power Map to plot the data right on flat and globe maps of the Earth. In Chapter 10, we will show you what's possible with Microsoft Power Map and Excel.

What You Need to Get Started

We assume you're relatively proficient with writing applications for Microsoft platforms. Ideally, you're a developer skilled with Microsoft technologies, and you've had some experience with C# and the .NET platform—with either native or server-side apps—and are comfortable using Microsoft Visual Studio. We're focused on making you proficient with the various location, mapping, and spatial facilities Microsoft puts at your disposal, rather than focusing on nuances of C# or building a native or web-based application. At the same time, if we're doing anything particularly clever with a language feature or an interface, we'll be sure to explain what we're doing and why, so you can benefit from our experience. Similarly, when we discuss the Bing Maps for iOS control, we assume you have some rudimentary iOS experience.

Of course, you'll also need a way to develop for Microsoft platforms if you want to build on Microsoft's technologies in your application. At a minimum, you'll need a copy of Microsoft Visual Studio. Visual Studio Express 2015 for Web is a good place to start for the web, and Visual Studio Express 2015 for Windows 10 for the native application development we will discuss later in this book.

We've written these chapters to be mostly independent of each other, stitched together by the common theme of this book and a collection of sample applications that demonstrate what we're helping you learn. On a first reading, a good start would be to read the remainder of this chapter, and then skip directly to the chapter that interests you the most.

A Few Words on Terminology

Before we continue, it's worth getting a few bits of terminology straight, because depending on where you look, you're going to see some vocabulary that may be unfamiliar.

First, we generally use the words *location*, *geospatial*, *spatial*, and *mapping* interchangeably when discussing the notion of adding geospatial data to an application. In the software industry, these words have settled into particular use in particular domains: Microsoft SQL Server's additions in 2008 included support for *geospatial* entities, for example, and you're going to see the word *mapping* appear a lot in the documentation for Bing Maps, while *location* is a frequently-occurring buzzword when it comes to how geospatial data is incorporated into social applications like Facebook, Twitter, and Foursquare.

Second, there are a few cartographic notions worth reviewing. Any position on the Earth can be represented as a pair of coordinates—a latitude, indicating how far north or south of the equator the point is, and a longitude, indicating how far east or west of the prime meridian (which falls through Greenwich, UK) the point is. By convention, northern latitudes are positive and southern latitudes are negative, while eastern longitudes are positive and western longitudes are negative. (Be careful! People in the western hemisphere new to geospatial software often assume that western longitude is positive. It isn't.)

The Earth is round, which poses some problems when we think about mapping it. First, our coordinate system breaks down at the poles and the International Date Line—at the poles, the latitude is +90 or -90, while all longitudes coexist at the actual poles. Perhaps more perplexing is what happens to longitude at the International Date Line; it's discontinuous there. At one point immediately to the west of the date line you'll have a longitude approaching +180; cross the line in an easterly direction and the sign flips, with a longitude of -180. This is one reason for Microsoft SQL Server's geography type—it takes these funky discontinuities in stride.

Another pitfall you're probably already aware of is that you can't present a flat map of the Earth on a plane without distortions. Various *projections* (consisting of formulas mapping a point on a sphere to a point on a plane) of the sphere onto the plane exist; Bing Maps, like most maps you're used to, uses the Mercator projection, which has two key advantages. It's conformal, meaning that the shape of relatively small objects is preserved. It's also cylindrical; at any point on the map, north and south are always up and down, and east and west are always left and right. However, the math of the projection gives some problems at the poles; Mercator maps don't map the pole regions very well, which is why when you look at countries further north and south from the equator, they look bigger in area than they actually are.

While the Earth is round, it's not perfectly round: it's a little squashed at the poles. To model the shape more exactly than using a sphere, geographers introduce the notion of the *datum*, a mathematical shape that more closely represents the Earth. To precisely position a point on the Earth, I should give you not just its latitude and longitude (and elevation, if the position is above or below the surface of the Earth), but also a reference to the datum the coordinates are in. Fortunately, nearly all systems today, including those you'll use from Microsoft and the positions returned by GPS receivers and cell phones, are in the World Geodetic System (WGS) 1984 datum, so you won't have to do any fancy math to move coordinates from one datum to another datum under normal circumstances.

■ **Note** Another datum you might encounter in your work is North American Datum 27 (NAD27), which is still in use by some U.S governmental agencies like the Federal Communications Commission. If you're plotting data from another source, it's crucial you find out what datum the coordinates are in and convert if necessary.

We touched on geocoding and reverse geocoding in a previous section as a feature of Bing Maps; to *geocode* a street address is to get the latitude and longitude for the street address, while to *reverse geocode* a latitude and longitude is to get the closest street address to the point. By their very nature, these are approximate transformations; in practice, you may find if you geocode an address and go to that point with a Global Positioning System (GPS) receiver that you're off by tens or hundreds of meters (even after taking into account the error in GPS), because addresses are often sequentially assigned to road segments assuming an equal spacing between addresses, rather than recognizing the nasty reality that parcel sizes may change, addresses may be skipped, and so on. If you're developing an application for another country, geocoding may be more or less accurate than it is in the United States because of how addresses get assigned; some on-location testing is probably in order.

Speaking of different countries, it's worth noting that some jurisdictions have very specific laws or regulations about what kids of geospatial information can be presented, recorded, or used. As of this writing, for example, there are restrictions in China both on where map data is stored (map providers like Microsoft must keep data about China in data centers inside China) and how the data can be presented on maps in software applications. If you're seeking to develop an application with international reach, or are specifically targeting one of those markets, you should stop and get the advice of a qualified legal professional early in your development cycle to make sure your business case meshes well with the legal climate.

Finally, this book is about writing software; the usual conventions apply for how you should read the print of the book. Words like this in a paragraph indicate a snippet of code such as a method or variable; when we present listings (which you don't need to type in, as the source code is available from the Apress website) to illustrate points, we'll set them out like this:

Listing 1-1. Hello World, in C#

```csharp
public class Hello
{
    public static void Main()
    {
        System.Console.WriteLine("Hello, World!");
    }
}
```

Introducing the Sample Application

It doesn't take much these days to come up with an application idea that can be improved by the judicious use of location—we think that's why you bought this book! Throughout the book, we hang most of our examples on a suite of sample applications based on the same use case: tracking and reporting statistics about earthquakes. We show you how to do this using the SQL Database service on Azure, hosting the service on Azure, and presenting the data using the Web, Windows Presentation Foundation (WPF) for Windows 7.0, and as a universal application for Windows 10, as well as showing the same data in Microsoft Power Map for Excel. In addition, we've created several smaller applications that show specific features of the Bing Maps API on specific clients, such as the reverse geocoding, routing, and traffic interfaces.

Before we dive into the next chapter and get you started with hosting your service on Azure, let's take a moment and look at the overall architecture for our main sample application; that way, as you read this book you will understand the fundamental points and can focus on the Microsoft mapping details along the way. Figures 1-2(a) and 1-2(b) show the WPF version of our sample application, first in its default state when launched and then after zooming in on a particular earthquake.

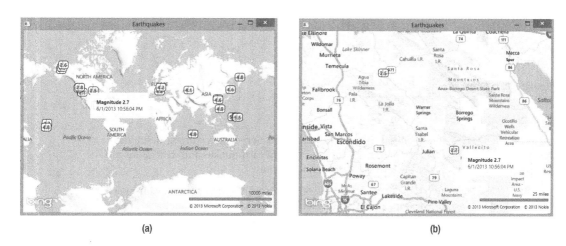

(a)   (b)

Figure 1-2. *Our sample application, in (a) showing the entire world, in (b) after zooming in using the scrollwheel or pinch-to-zoom to see a particular area*

The sample application is intentionally simple; its sole purpose is to provide a map populated with recent earthquakes around the world. You'll see this example again and again in this book, first as an application for the web and later as a native application for WPF, and then as a universal application for Windows 10. (You'll also see chunks of other sample applications that demonstrate other Bing Maps features such as traffic layers, routing, and geocoding.) When you launch the application, it immediately draws a map of the world and fetches recent earthquake data from our Azure service; you can zoom in on any area, pan the map, or hover over a marker to get more information about a specific earthquake record.

Figure 1-3 shows a block diagram of the overall architecture we've chosen for this sample application. It's admittedly more than the back end our earthquake-monitoring client requires, but it lets us share with you important details about setting up services for location-based applications, hosting on Windows Azure, writing applications that communicate between client and server, and, of course, the client applications themselves.

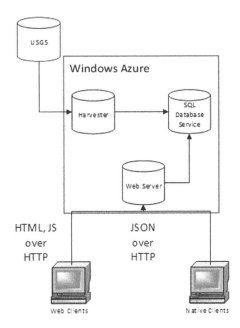

Figure 1-3. *The architecture for our sample application*

The components you see are:

- The USGS. It provides the raw earthquake data. Served as a comma-delimited file (CSV) over HTTP, each file contains a list of earthquakes and data about each earthquake over the last twenty-four hour period.

- The Harvester. It is a process running on Windows Azure that periodically polls the USGS for earthquake data and inserts records into the SQL database. (In a production application, it might also perform work such as purging the database of old records, or that might be left to other maintenance processes).

- The SQL database storing our earthquake data. It runs on the Azure SQL Database Service as a single database, with rows for each earthquake harvested by the harvester.

- The web server, running in Microsoft IIS. It serves both the HTML and JavaScript for web clients using the service and provides a Windows Communication Foundation (WCF) service serving the same data to both web and native clients using JavaScript Object Notation (JSON) over the HyperText Transfer Protocol (HTTP).

- Application clients. These come in two flavors: web and native. The web client loads its application directly from the web server as JavaScript, with HTML and image resources. The native clients run locally on a Windows 7, Windows 8, or Windows 10 host (either Windows for the desktop or Windows Phone, as it's a Windows Universal application). All clients use the same WCF bindings, making integration simple for the Windows applications, and only a little more difficult for the iOS platforms.

It's worth taking a few minutes to explain why we chose this architecture. First, there are more pieces than you'd need just to browse earthquake data from the USGS; you could just as easily pull the data directly from the USGS and display it on a map with Power Maps, which is what we will do in Chapter 10. This is a reasonable approach, but not sufficient for our purposes, where we hope to show you how to build and deploy a Windows Azure service for your application.

In a real production service, your entire web service may live on Azure, or you may be dependent on legacy or enterprise services running in another data center. If that's the case, you need to bridge the gap somehow. We chose to bridge this gap using our harvester process, because one of our goals is to show you how to use the geospatial features in Microsoft's various database products. Our harvester polls the USGS and inserts earthquake records into our database; your bridge may do something similar, replicating an existing database. More likely—and more efficiently—your bridge running on Azure can make web service calls to your legacy services, leaving the database on Azure for your client-specific operations not related to the legacy service. (In fact, your legacy server might also be a Microsoft SQL Server instance of some kind, and you might choose to host your geospatial data there.)

For large-scale services, you should consider replicating your SQL server on multiple hosts, either in your enterprise data center or in different zones of Microsoft Azure. We don't explicitly discuss replication in this book; for that, you should consult any of the good books on Microsoft SQL Server administration. However, it's important to recognize that the database can be a single point of failure for your entire service, so distributing this asset is a key component when building a large-scale service.

Equally important is distributing the front end to your service. As we will discuss in the next chapter when we explore Windows Azure in more detail, Azure has the notion of web hosts and worker hosts. Our harvester runs on a worker host, an instance of a machine responsible for doing batch computation, rather than serving client endpoints. In production environments, you'd replicate the web host providing the front-end services multiple times, placing them behind one of Azure's load balancers that is configured to distribute client requests among multiple hosts. When you do this, you need to remember that client-server requests should be *stateless*; that is, they should be atomic and not rely on a persistent connection or sequence. This lets the load balancer make the most of your service, and ensures that if a web server goes down (or its connection is interrupted during the course of normal services) the failover to another service can happen with a minimum of difficulty and no sign to the user that a transaction failed.

What kind of clients you choose for your application is largely a business decision. In our case, we wanted to show you the full range of platforms that Bing Maps supports, so we wrote clients for the web as well as the native clients that can host a Bing Maps control. Enterprise developers may choose to only support one or two platforms: say a native application using WPF or the web, and a universal application for mobile workers running on Windows Phone. If you're exclusively targeting Windows, you have an important decision to make: Do you ship your application through the Windows Store and focus on Windows 10 users, or do you package your application and distribute it yourself, likely as a WPF application that runs on Windows 7 and Windows 8? Or do you do both, providing legacy Windows 7 users a means to access your service as well as supporting the more modern user-interface paradigms in Windows 10? This decision is tricky, and likely will involve both programmers (who provide the cost estimates to build and maintain all of these applications) and business people (who should have an understanding of your target market and what platforms your prospective customers are actually using).

Developing Your Application

Developing a location-aware application is similar in process to developing any application. If your development team is small, or a one-man operation, be prepared to wear a lot of hats: database administrator, web service developer, client application developer. If you're building a larger application, or are part of a team, a good way to divide and conquer the application development space is to partition it into three broad teams: *content*, *cloud*, and *client*:

- The content team is responsible for identifying and capturing any content your application needs. For example, if your application is a restaurant table reservation service, this team is responsible for identifying the restaurants you serve (likely a sales function) as well as developing the database schema and database for that content. Or maybe you're writing a location-aware game and need to capture locations that provide the setting and environment of the game; in that case, the content team is responsible for determining what data is germane to each setting, how it's stored, and so forth. You'll want content and database experts working together on this team.

- The cloud team builds the web services necessary to support the clients. It reaches into the content database over a well-defined interface to get what it needs on the one side, and serves that content to clients through a well-defined interface (likely WCF-hosted) on the other. Developers on this team should have good understanding of Azure and service deployment, and be able to write server-side applications fluently.

- The client team builds the clients that use the cloud team's web service. The responsibilities of this team vary depending on the kind of clients you need to support; maybe all you need is a crackerjack ASP.NET programmer and a good webpage designer, or maybe you need native application development teams to target a number of platforms.

Dividing your work this way makes sense even if you're a small team; you can change roles depending on the phase of development you're in or what needs doing that day. It's easier to think about the complexities of a location-based application if you break down the pieces into manageable chunks, and these three chunks give you a good place to start. Of course, a larger effort may have multiple teams in each category; maybe you've got different client teams targeting the web, Apple iOS, and Windows Phone. Or maybe you're in the business of producing a lot of content (think of a service like Yelp) with sophisticated requirements for collecting and storing the content your service offers.

We're big fans of agile development, with one caveat: you need to take some care in defining the interfaces between each portion of your application, and spend some time up front making sure that you have a good database architecture in hand. In some software companies, *agile* is a substitute for *no design*; we prefer a model where small design tasks (say, identifying the interfaces the client will use to connect to the cloud) are estimated just the same as software tasks, and some lightweight documentation should accompany the final product. A model like scrum works particularly well for this, as you can iteratively refine each functional area if you're a small team in successive sprints, or run simultaneous scrum teams for each functional area at the same time, and then integrate the results with integration sprints between developing your core features.

Wrapping Up

While many firms provide the pieces you need to assemble a location-aware application for the web, desktop, or mobile client, only Microsoft offers an end-to-end solution that includes

- a database (Microsoft SQL Server) with geospatial support for flat-map and round-Earth coordinate systems, capable of storing and querying points and regions;

- a PaaS (Windows Azure) for hosting your database (using Azure's SQL Database Service) and cloud computing requirements, including state-of-the-art web hosting with Microsoft IIS;

- client-side map-rendering controls (Bing Maps) for the web, WPF, and Windows Universal applications, and

- web services to support your application, including traffic, routing, geocoding, and reverse geocoding features.

The remainder of this book will show you how you can build your application with each of these pieces, giving you the skills you need to make your own location-aware applications. In the next chapter, we'll dig into Windows Azure, so fasten your seat belt and prepare to take off into the cloud!

CHAPTER 2

■ ■ ■

Painless Hosting with Azure

In this chapter we will show you how to host a simple application that displays a Bing Map on Microsoft Azure (formerly Windows Azure), Microsoft's cloud-computing platform. Cloud computing provides agile IT for businesses and developers. If a business wanted to deploy a new web application, the traditional method of deployment would require that the business set up the necessary hardware, software, operations, and support team in order to host this application on premises. With cloud computing, all of the infrastructure needed to deploy that application would already be available on the cloud, thereby reducing the necessary setup time and money required to deploy.

Why Microsoft Azure?

The main benefit of moving to the cloud is the savings in time and infrastructure for application deployment. You can focus on your application development and not the infrastructure. The backend is fully automated and handles the patching, updating, and maintenance of the operating system and applications. Microsoft Azure follows a pay-per-use model, where you only pay for the resources that your application uses; there is no upfront cost. One major concern in application deployment is the ability to survive hardware and system failures, and Microsoft Azure is designed with high availability in mind. Applications are replicated across multiple servers in different locations for fail-safe recovery. Microsoft delivers a 99.95% monthly SLA (Service-Level Agreement).

As is often the goal, your application may at times require scaling up as demands grow. Microsoft Azure is designed for elastic scale; therefore, multiple instances can be spun up as needed. Alternatively, the customer can drop the number of instances to zero when there is no demand. Since Microsoft Azure follows the pay-per-use model, you only pay for the number of instances that you use and the storage you consume. Another important benefit is that SQL Database (formerly SQL Azure), which is the storage component of Microsoft Azure, shares basic programming models with Microsoft SQL Server; thus, if you are familiar with the SQL Server product code base, your skills can be applied to working with SQL Database.

While a relatively new business for Microsoft, the growth of Microsoft Azure is a testament to the growing importance of cloud computing as well as of Microsoft's platform. Microsoft announced that as of April 2013, Microsoft Azure had crossed the $1 billion threshold (see `http://bloom.bg/10JDhtG`), with over 200,000 customers. Although Microsoft does not disclose its revenues from Azure, it is estimated that Azure experienced roughly 136% annual growth rates in 2014 (`http://bloom.bg/1GCiZT4`) and is continuing to grow at an accelerated pace with over 10,000 new customers signed to Azure per week (`http://onforb.es/1JaiF29`).

Cloud-Computing Services

Cloud computing refers to the notion of placing computing services in a central data center, accessible by the Internet. The main types of cloud-computing services are Infrastructure as a Service (IaaS), Platform as a Service (PaaS), and Software as a Service (SaaS).

- IaaS provides the hardware necessary for deploying an application; however, the onus is on the developer (customer) to patch, upgrade, and maintain the operating system.

- With PaaS, in addition to the hardware, the operating system and runtime environment necessary for deploying an application are also provided.

- Finally, SaaS provides the entire end-to-end software application to the customer. The customer is only required to sign up for a given service, and the SaaS handles the entire application.

We should note that there are, in fact, other types of cloud services such as Security as a Service or IT as a Service offered by other cloud-computing platforms. The types of services available with Microsoft Azure are virtual machines (VMs) (IaaS), cloud-application services (PaaS), and websites (SaaS), as shown in Figure 2-1.

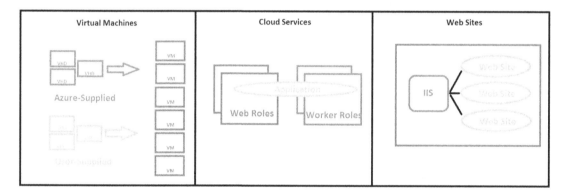

Figure 2-1. *Compute services offered by Microsoft Azure*

Virtual Machines (IaaS)

Rather than requiring an actual on-premises physical machine, you can create VMs on demand—either from an image you supply or from a standard image. To create a VM, you simply specify which virtual hard disk (VHD) to use and the size of the VM. Once you've done that, you can define a VM role for your application. Essentially, Azure provides you with a server in the cloud that you can control and manage. You can deploy any available instance of Windows Server or Linux. Each VM will have your virtual hard desk (VHD), and it can contain your customized settings as well as your applications. You can make changes to these settings and applications while a VM is running, and the change is persisted such that the next time you create a VM from that VHD, the changes will be reflected. Alternatively, you can copy the changed VHD out of the cloud and run it locally.

There are different ways in which Microsoft Azure VMs can be used. First, you can use them to create inexpensive development and test platforms. Additionally, you can create and run applications that use any of the data-management options provided by Microsoft Azure in conjunction with either SQL Server or another DBMS running in your VM. Finally, you can even use VMs as an extension of an on-premises data center. Microsoft Azure's VMs, in essence, provide the highest level of flexibility for those who would like to have access to many machines and full control of their management.

Cloud Services (PaaS)

A slightly less flexible service is a cloud service. In this case, you are given full control over your application; however, you are exempt from the work required for administration. Applications can be deployed in Azure using languages such as C#, Java, PHP, Python, or Node.js in a VM that is running a version of Windows Server. To clarify, with the VMs described in the previous subsection, you must define the VM infrastructure, while with cloud services, you are given a predefined VM on which you can deploy your applications. Azure will handle all of the management of this VM, including restarting any VMs that fail.

There are two types of roles to choose from for cloud services: web and worker roles. A web role is for a front-end/web server. For example, you might have an ASP.NET-enabled website. In this case, you use the web role and upload the website code to the cloud. Azure will automatically deploy the website to the Azure Virtual Machine (VM) instances and provide load balancing between the instances you've created.

Websites (SaaS)

Offering the least amount of flexibility are the SaaS Microsoft Azure Websites. This service allows you to build a scalable website using any operating system and ASP.NET, PHP, or Node.js and then deploy this website on the cloud. You manage the web environment using Microsoft Internet Information Service (IIS). You can either create a new website directly in the cloud or move an existing IIS website onto Microsoft Azure, as we will do in the example in this chapter. You can have multiple instances of the website running, and you can remove or add these instances even as the website is running. Additionally, Azure allows you to load balance the requests to the website across the various instances for higher performance.

As you have just read, Microsoft Azure provides you with the types of services that you can tailor to your needs. In fact, you can use one, two, or all three of these types of services in conjunction with each other depending on your needs. Moreover, at all times Microsoft Azure has focused on providing a highly reliable cloud solution. As such, your VMs and applications are spread out across various locations and replicated for redundancy to safeguard against hardware failures and other such disasters.

At times you may want to have parts of your solution hosted on Azure but the remainder of it on premises. The *AppFabric* is the glue that connects these parts together by allowing you to integrate the Microsoft Azure applications with the on-premises application. You can leverage the *Service Bus* to enable communication between the cloud and on-premises applications. Alternatively, you can use the AppFabric's *Access Control Service* to create highly secure authorization for applications. Essentially, the AppFabric is a framework for managing and monitoring the applications running in the cloud.

Microsoft Azure Data Management

Azure also offers data services that allow you to store your data on the cloud. As you can see in Figure 2-2, the types of storage options are blobs, tables, and SQL databases. They are accessible via REST API calls or standard HTTP calls. Before we describe each of these types of storage, it is important to note that once again Microsoft Azure allows you to only pay for the amount of storage you use per month. Moreover, while the storage can be accessed by your Azure applications, it can also be accessed by applications running on your own local machines.

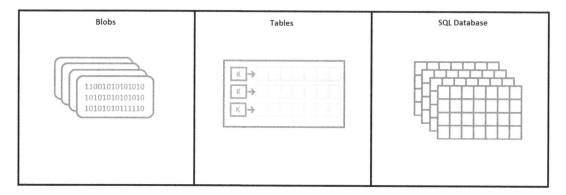

Figure 2-2. *Microsoft Azure offers different types of data storage: blobs, tables, and SQL databases*

Blobs

Blobs (**B**inary **L**arge **Ob**jects) are unstructured text or binary data such as images, audio, or videos. This type of storage is inexpensive, and a single blob can be as large as one terabyte. Blobs are grouped into containers, and your account can have an unlimited number of containers; each container can contain an unlimited number of blobs. The only restriction is that the total size of all blobs must be less than 100 TBs for a single storage account. In Figure 2-3, there are nine blobs in that one account, of which there are three types of containers (image, audio, and video), and five distinct containers.

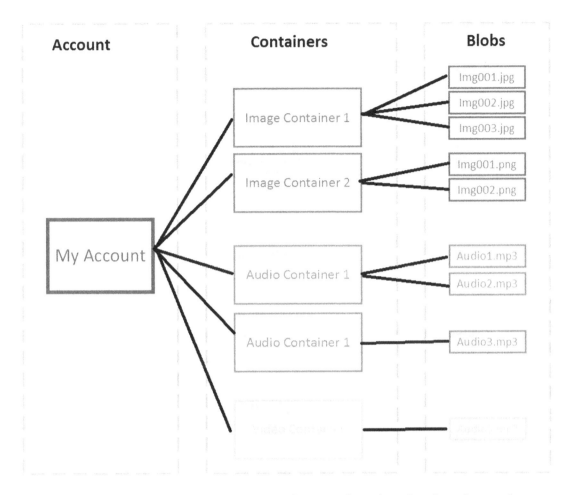

Figure 2-3. *Example of blob storage. Each account can have an unlimited number of containers, and containers can contain an unlimited number of blobs of the same type*

Tables

Tables contain large amounts of structured but non-relational data, as shown in Figure 2-4. For example, you may wish to store a large amount of data that does not require you to perform SQL queries on it, but that you would still like to be able to access quickly. In this case, tables are a good choice for data storage. Groups of data, such as dates, can be accessed by a key that is unique to that group. This type of storage is far less expensive than SQL databases, but still provides you with the ability to randomly access your data quickly.

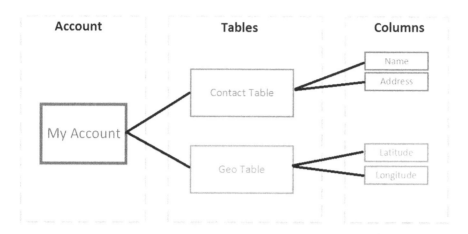

Figure 2-4. *Table storage in Azure is for non-relational data. An account can have from 0 to n tables associated with it*

SQL Databases

Finally, SQL databases are large amounts of structured and relational data. If you are familiar with using SQL Server, then you are familiar with SQL Database. As with SQL Server, SQL Database can be accessed using a variety of data-access tools such as ADO.NET or JDBC. SQL Database offers the added advantage of being a PaaS, in that while you can control the data and who can access it, Microsoft Azure takes care of managing all the hardware and infrastructure for you. Additionally, SQL Database federates the data across multiple servers, which is particularly useful for performance if your database receives large quantities of access requests.

In our example in this book, we will be storing blobs of geo data on the cloud. For the moment, in this chapter's example we will simply deploy an ASP.NET MVC on Azure.

Setting Up Microsoft Azure

Getting started with Microsoft Azure is easy. You'll sign up for an account, download the Microsoft Azure SDK to your computer so you can use Microsoft Visual Studio to develop your Microsoft Azure applications, and that's it!

As you use the Microsoft Azure SDK, you can also model most of the Microsoft Azure features, including storage and hosting, right on your local development machine. This is especially handy when you're just starting development, because it lets you experiment with Microsoft Azure and your code without taking the time to spin up one or more virtual machines to host your services.

Getting a Microsoft Azure Account

Before you can begin developing your application, you will need a Microsoft Azure account. Microsoft has made this a painless, straightforward process. You can begin with signing up for a trial at `http://bit.ly/15tpYgF` (`http://azure.microsoft.com/`, formerly `http://windowsazure.com`), as shown in Figure 2-5, with a single click. Click on Try For Free.

Figure 2-5. *Microsoft Azure website provides a straightforward way of signing up for a free trial and account*

■ **Note** Microsoft experiments with different trial offers; when we wrote this, the trial was a one-month free trial. Your mileage may vary, however, and if you're a member of MSDN, there may be a MSDN trial available as well.

You will be required to sign in with a Windows Live ID, which you can also sign up for at (http://signup.live.com, http://bit.ly/1Ii9kqq) if you do not yet have one. Once you have signed in, you will be redirected to the one-month free trial page, as shown in Figure 2-6. After clicking Try It Now, you will need both a mobile phone as well as a credit card for signing up. You will not be charged on your credit card during the trial, as it's just for verification and as a means for Microsoft to avoid spam botting. You will begin by entering a mobile phone number, to which a verification code will be sent. Once you verify your account with the code, you will be asked for your credit card information. After entering your credit card information, your sign-in is complete.

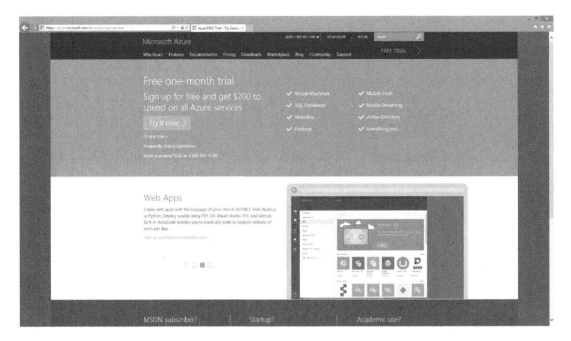

Figure 2-6. *Microsoft Azure one-month free trial sign-up page*

Getting the Microsoft Azure SDK

Now that you've obtained a Microsoft Azure Account, you will want to install the Microsoft Azure SDK on your development machine. In this book, we will be using Visual Studio 2015 ASP.NET, and C#. Of course, ASP.NET is not the only web-hosting language you can use with Microsoft Azure. Figure 2-7 shows the different SDKs you can install on your machine for development, which you can reach by clicking Documentation on the drop-down menu on the dashboard, as seen in Figure 2-8. Click on .NET to install the SDK. You will be given the option of installing the SDK for VS 2012, 2013, and even 2015. If your machine already has an older version of Visual Studio installed, that is also acceptable, but be sure to install the corresponding SDK when given the option. Alternatively, if your machine does not have Visual Studio installed, the one-click installation will also install the Web Express edition on your machine.

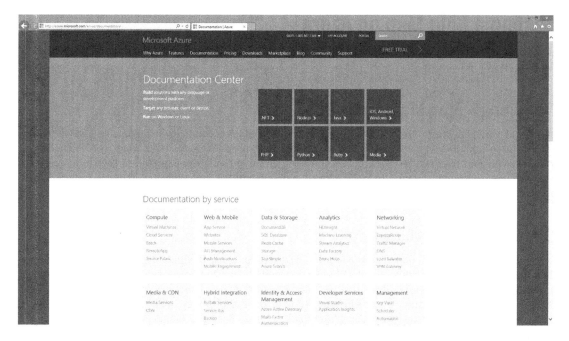

Figure 2-7. *The Microsoft Azure website provides easy one-click installation for various SDKs for Microsoft Azure development*

Figure 2-8. *The Microsoft Azure dashboard*

Hosting a Bing Map on Azure

To make sure you've set everything up correctly, let's create a simple webpage that just shows a map using the Bing Maps AJAX control.

Obtaining a Bing Maps Account

In order to work with Bing Maps, you will need to obtain Bing Maps account, if you do not already have one. You can do so at `http://bit.ly/ZmFU3q` (`https://www.bingmapsportal.com`). Once again, you will need to sign in with your Windows Live ID account. Once you do so, you will need to provide an account name, a contact name, a company name, an email address, a phone number, and agree to the Bing Maps terms of use. Once you have saved this information, you now have a Bing Maps Account.

Obtaining a Bing Maps Key

Even though you have an account, you still require a key in order to use the Bing Maps API. You can do so at the same site from which you obtained the Bing Maps account. If you are not already signed in, you will be prompted to sign in with your Windows Live ID. Once you do so, you can obtain a key by clicking on Create or View Keys under My Account. You will be required to fill out the form seen in Figure 2-9. The application name is required, as well as the type of key. In this book, we use a Basic key, which is used for non-trial applications that do not exceed 50,000 transactions of any type within a 24-hour period. A Basic key must comply with the Bings Maps Terms of Use, which you can read at `http://bit.ly/16Bx1bS` (`https://www.microsoft.com/maps/product/terms.html`).

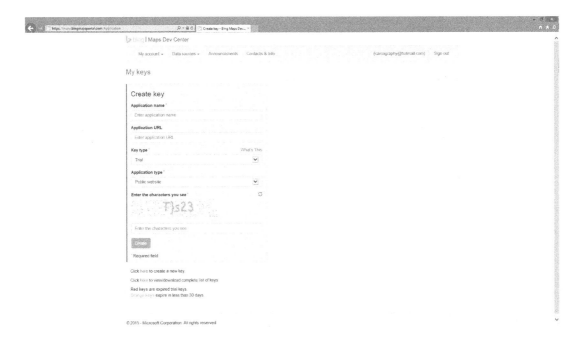

Figure 2-9. *Obtain a key to work with the Bing Maps API by creating a key at* `www.bingmapsportal.com`

Once you submit the Create Key form, you will then have a key you can use with the Bing Maps API. It should be a 64-character string. For example:

ABCDEFGHIJKLMNOPQRSTUVWXYZ1234567890abcdefghijklmnopqrstuvwxyz12

■ **Note** Make sure you stick a copy of your Bing Maps Key someplace handy, as you'll need it a lot when working through the sample code in this book. Although, you can always create a new key if necessary!

With this string you are now ready to use the Bing Maps API to build your sample application.

Building the Bing Map

Now that you have a Bing Map API key, you are ready to begin using the Bing Map API to build your map. Microsoft offers a Bing Map API interactive SDK at the Bing Maps portal: `http://bit.ly/18HDak6`. From this portal, you can choose the types of features you would like to add to your map and get the corresponding HTML code listing to create such a map by clicking on View HTML, as seen in Figure 2-10.

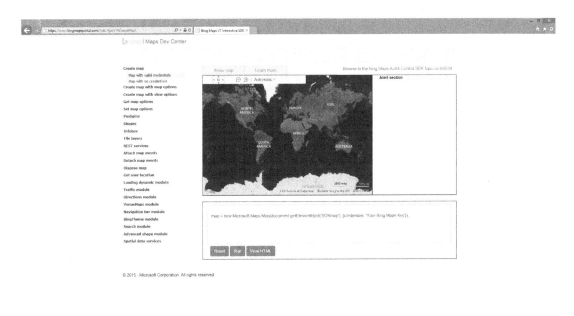

Figure 2-10. *Bing Map API Interactive SDK provides support for map creation*

For our example, we use the basic map with the correct credentials. The credential is the Bing Map key we obtained in the previous section. You will replace the string `Your Bing Maps Key` with the key. Thus, your HTML listing will look like the code in Listing 2-1. You will then be able to save this listing as an HTML file and view it in a browser. We have saved this listing as `Map.htm`. This map has basic zoom functionality as well as the option to switch between road and aerial (Bird's Eye) view.

Listing 2-1. Map.htm, HTML code for a basic Bing Map with valid credentials

```
<!DOCTYPE html PUBLIC "-//W3C//DTD XHTML 1.0 Transitional//EN"
"http://www.w3.org/TR/xhtml1/DTD/xhtml1-transitional.dtd">
<html>
    <head>
        <title>Map with valid credentials</title>
        <meta http-equiv="Content-Type" content="text/html; charset=utf-8"/>
        <script
            type="text/javascript"
            src="http://ecn.dev.virtualearth.net/mapcontrol/mapcontrol.ashx?v=7.0">
        </script>
        <script type="text/javascript">
        var map = null;
        function getMap()
        {
            map = new Microsoft.Maps.Map(document.getElementById('myMap'),
            {
                credentials: 'ABCDEFGHIJKLMNOPQRSTUVWXYZ1234567890abcdefghijklmnopqrstuvwxyz12'
            });
        }
        </script>
    </head>
    <body onload="getMap();">
        <div id='myMap' style="position:relative; width:400px; height:400px;"></div>
    </body>
</html>
```

Hosting the Bing Map on Microsoft Azure

Now that you have created the map, we will show you how to programmatically host it on Microsoft Azure.

In Visual Studio 2015, create a new ASP.NET web application project for C#, as shown in Figure 2-11. We save the project as BingMapOnAzure.

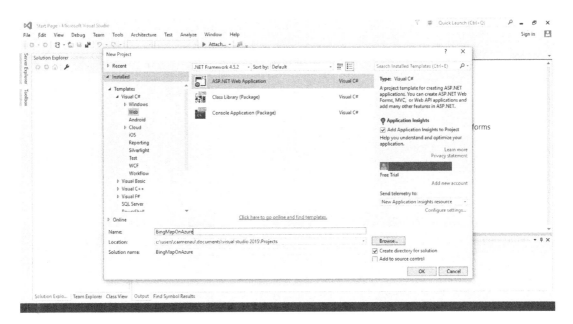

Figure 2-11. *Visual Studio 2012, create a ASP .NET web application*

Select the MVC template, like in Figure 2-12. This template generates the code for creating a basic MVC web application. You could alternatively select an Empty template, which provides the bare minimum of folders and files; however, you will then forgo the authentication options. The MVC template provides all the controls you will need for a website that is rich in UI and follows the Model-View-Controller pattern. From this page, you will also be asked to sign in to Azure so you can host your webpage on the cloud, as shown in Figure 2-13. Make sure the "Host in the cloud" box is checked. You can also change authentication to one of the following four options: No Authentication, Individual User Accounts, Work and School Accounts, and Windows Authentication. For simplicity, we have chosen the No Authentication option. Once you have created your application, you can run it, and it will produce the webpage in Figure 2-14.

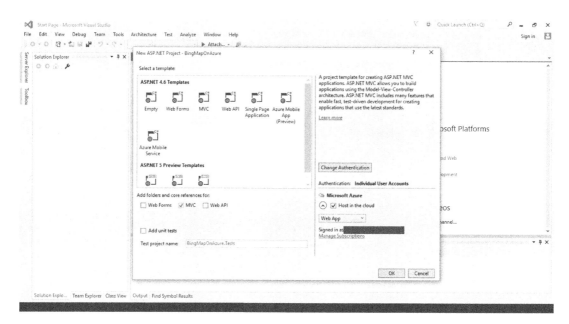

Figure 2-12. *There's a variety of templates to choose from, including the MVC template we use in this chapter*

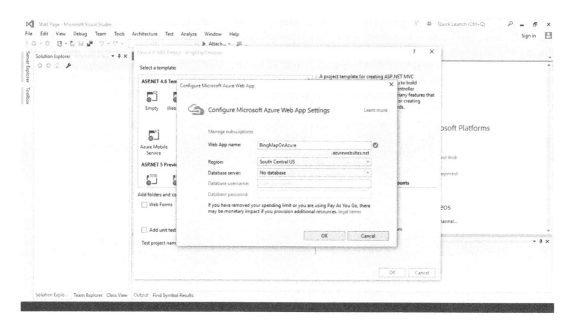

Figure 2-13. *Microsoft Azure web app configuration form*

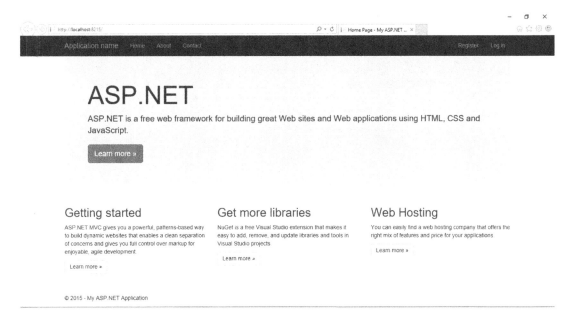

Figure 2-14. *Basic MVC web application webpage generated by the code template from Visual Studio*

We will now modify this template code to host the Bing map generated in the previous section. In the current template, there are different tabbed pages: Home, About, and Contact. We will modify the map over the About page. First, in the listing, you will change the name of the page from About to Map in both the code listing and the About.cshtml file name to Map.cshtml in the Solution Explorer, as in Figure 2-15.

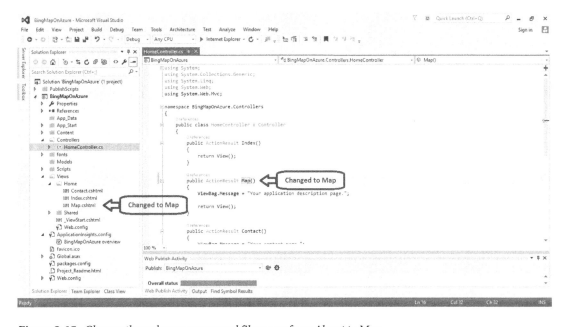

Figure 2-15. *Change the webpage name and file name from About to Map*

In _Layout.cshtml, change the action link parameters from About to Map; see Figure 2-16.

Figure 2-16. *Change the link About to Map*

In Map.cshtml, paste the Bing map code listing from Listing 2-1, as shown in Figure 2-17. Change the width and height of the resulting map as desired. We have selected 1000px and 500px for this example.

Figure 2-17. *Map.cshtml with Bing map code listing from Listing 2-1*

When we created the project, we already enabled the webpage to be deployed or published to Azure. In fact, if you go to bingmaponazure.azurewebsites.net, you will see the following message in Figure 2-18. In order to see the webpage you have just created, you need to publish it to Azure.

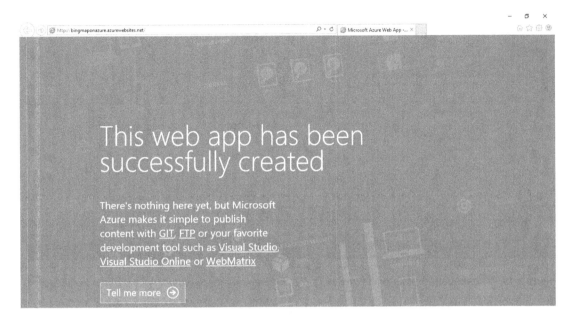

Figure 2-18. To Azure-enable the project, right-click on Add Microsoft Azure Cloud Service Project

To publish, right-click on the project name in the Solution Explorer and select publish (see Figure 2-19). Hosting, Bing Map:Publish Web form You will then be brought to the Publish Web Form seen in Figure 2-20. Once you've verified that all your credentials and settings are correct, click Publish.

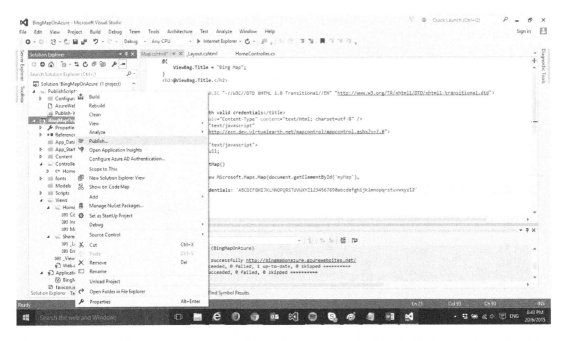

Figure 2-19. *To publish the webpage to Azure, right-click on project in the Solution Explorer and select Publish*

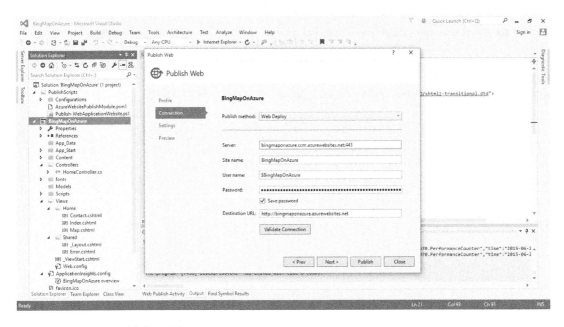

Figure 2-20. *Azure Publish Web form*

■ **Note** You will need to be signed in to your Windows Live account to publish to Azure.

The resulting application that is running on Azure will open in the web browser. Figure 2-21 shows the Bing Map application running in a web browser. If you forgot to check the "Host in the cloud" box when you were creating this solution, you can always still click Publish like in Figure Hosting, Bing Map:webpage creation Figure 2-22. However, instead of the resulting Azure Publish Web form, you will be presented a form that lets you select the Microsoft Azure Web App as the publish target, which looks like Figure 2-23. You can then name your web app with a unique name and click Create and then Publish to publish to the cloud.

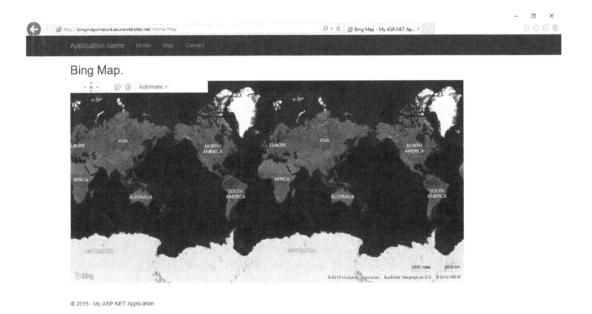

Figure 2-21. Bing Map application

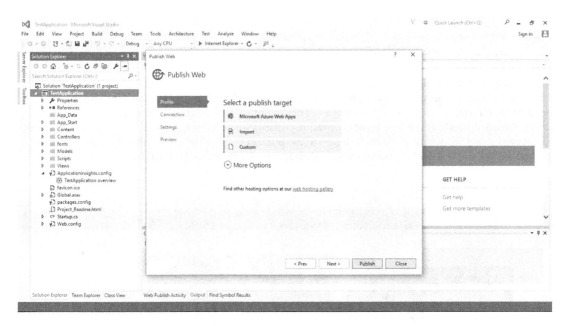

Figure 2-22. *Select the Microsoft Azure Web Apps target to publish to the web*

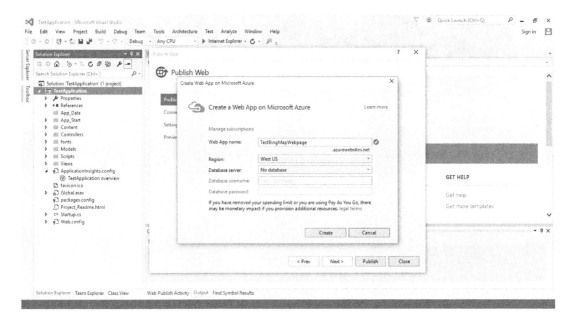

Figure 2-23. *Select a unique web app name and click Create to create the webpage*

Wrapping Up

In this chapter, we learned about hosting on Microsoft Azure. Microsoft Azure is a robust, easy-to-install, cost-effective solution for those looking to manage their own virtual machines in the cloud, deploy applications while leaving the management of the operating system to Azure, or simply host websites in the cloud. Using a cloud-based solution, you can avoid all the costs associated with hosting things on-premises, such as hardware, infrastructure, and support team. Additionally, Azure follows a pay-per-use model, where you only pay for what you use, thereby significantly reducing costs. Azure also was built with reliability and robustness in mind. Your data and applications are replicated over several servers in various different physical locations to protect you from any hardware failures or other disasters that could occur. The other advantage of Azure is the ease of use. Installation is done in a single click! Any developer who is familiar with .NET is already primed for programming to deploy in Azure. Alternatively, you can also develop in Node.js or even PHP.

The example in this chapter showed you how to install Microsoft Azure, obtain a Bing Maps Key, build a Bing Map in .NET, and finally deploy this map on Azure. In the following chapter, we will show you how to get your geospatial data onto the Azure storage and how to manage this data.

■ ■ ■

CHAPTER 3

Geospatial Data with Azure SQL Database

In this chapter, we will give you a brief overview of Azure's SQL Database and how it can be used to host your geospatial data. We will then present a sample application that takes the geospatial earthquake data from http://earthquake.usgs.gov/earthquakes/ and stores it on the SQL Database.

SQL Database Overview

If you are familiar with SQL Server, transitioning to Azure SQL Database will be straightforward, as the latter is just the cloud-based implementation of a relational database that is built on top of Microsoft SQL Server. You will find that SQL Database is referred to as SQL Azure in many books and online resources. For all intents and purposes, they are one and the same, and you can think of SQL Azure as the former name of SQL Database, and SQL Database as the updated version of SQL Azure.

There are a few key differences between SQL Server and SQL Database. SQL Server is hosted on-premises, and you are responsible for the administration of both the database and the physical hardware. SQL Database abstracts the logical from the physical administration, so you are only responsible for the administration of the databases, logins, users, and roles. Hardware, such as the hard drives, servers, and storage, is all taken care of by Microsoft Azure. In addition to removing the responsibility of obtaining and maintaining hardware, the benefit of using SQL Database over SQL Server is that you have access to a service that is highly scalable, highly available, highly secure, and highly reliable. Scalability is made possible because SQL Database enables you to spin up as many virtual machines as you require. Availability is made possible because SQL Database handles the load balancing for you. And security and reliability are possible because SQL Database replicates your data across different locations, and Microsoft Azure automatically handles the security for you.

Your databases may reside on different physical computers at the Microsoft data center. Because your data is automatically replicated, and you do not have access to the computers' file systems, the SQL Server backup and restore commands are not applicable to SQL Database. You are, however, permitted to copy your entire database to a new database in SQL Database. With on-premises SQL Server setups, you are responsible for preparing the server with the appropriate systems, data, and software to make it ready for network operation. SQL Database handles this provisioning process for you. And you can begin this process immediately after you create your Microsoft Azure account.

Accessing Data in SQL Database

There are two ways of accessing data in the SQL Database, as seen in Figure 3-1:

- Application is hosted on-premises and uses Tabular Data Stream (TDS) over a secure sockets layer (SSL) to transfer data from the SQL Database.

- Application is hosted on Microsoft Azure, and the database also resides on Microsoft Azure. This is the scenario we are using in this chapter. You will use a web-based client and the WCF Data Services to access the application and data hosted on Azure.

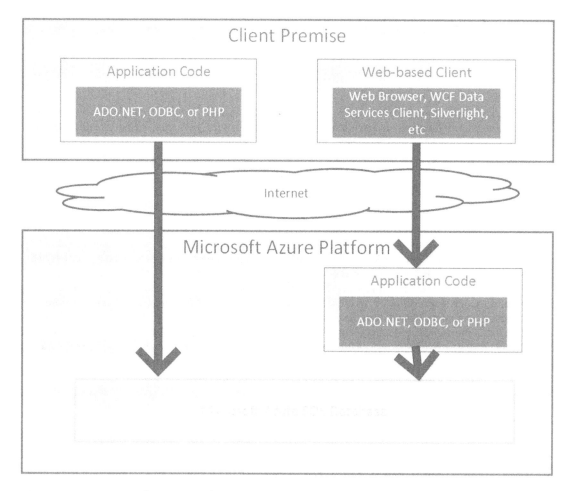

Figure 3-1. *Two options for accessing data in the SQL Database: application code is on-premises, or application code is in the cloud*

Both options are viable, but come with different implications. When you host your application on-premises, one major issue is network latency. Traditionally, both your application and your server would be hosted on-premises; however, if you move your server to the cloud, then you must consider the latency of trafficking the data between the server and the application. By hosting both your application and your database in Azure, you minimize the network latency of requests to the database.

SQL Database Architecture Overview

The SQL Database architecture is divided into four layers: the client layer, the service layer, the platform layer, and the infrastructure layer. Figure 3-2 shows these layers.

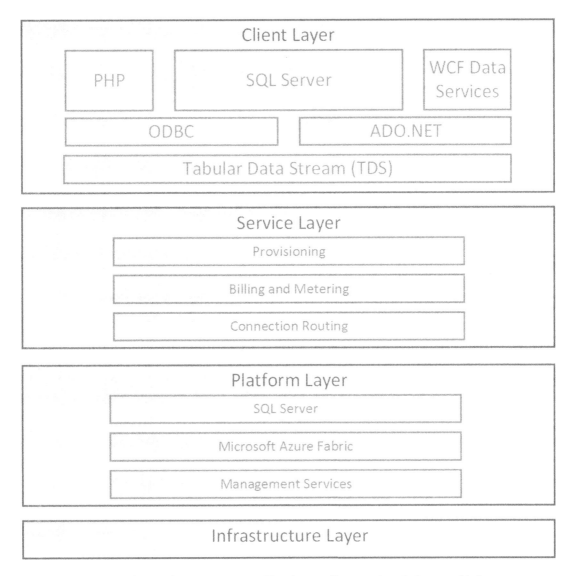

Figure 3-2. *SQL Database architecture consists of four layers: client, service, platform, and infrastructure*

The Client Layer

The client layer can reside either on-premises or on Azure. This is the layer that is closest to your application. SQL Database provides the same tabular data stream (TDS) interface as SQL Server does; thus, the tools and libraries are familiar, if you are familiar with SQL Server.

The Service Layer

The service layer provides three functions: provisioning, billing and metering, and connection routing.

- **Provisioning**: Provisions the databases with the necessary systems, data, and software so that the database is ready for network use.

- **Billing and metering**: The billing and metering is what monitors each Microsoft Azure account's usage. This service is what allows multi-tenant support on SQL Database.

- **Connection routing**: Your data may reside on numerous physical servers. The service layer is what handles all the connections between your application and your data on the various servers.

The Platform Layer

The platform layer is where your data resides. It consists of many SQL Server instances, each of which is managed by the SQL Database fabric. The SQL Database fabric is a distributed computing system made up of tightly integrated networks, servers, and storage. It handles the load balancing, automatic failover, and automatic replication of data between servers.

The Infrastructure Level

The infrastructure level handles the IT administration of the physical hardware and operating systems that support the services layer.

SQL Database Provisioning Model

As seen in Figure 3-3, a Microsoft Azure platform can be associated with multiple SQL Database servers, and a SQL Database server can be associated with multiple databases.

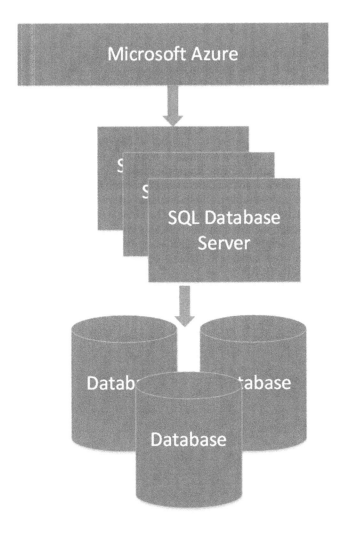

Figure 3-3. *SQL provisioning model: Each Azure platform is associated with multiple servers, and each server can be associated with multiple databases*

A SQL Database server is a logical group of databases and handles the administration between multiple databases. The SQL Database server includes logins similar to those in instances of SQL Server. During the provisioning process, each SQL Database server is assigned a unique domain name, such as *servername. database.windows.net*, where *servername* is the name of the SQL Database server.

The databases are what contain the data and use tables, views, indices, and other stored procedures. During the provisioning process, a master database is created, and it keeps track of which logins have permission to create databases or other logins. You must be connected to **master** (the database created in the provisioning process) in order to CREATE, ALTER, or DROP logins.

Federations in SQL Database

A *federation* is a collection of database partitions, which are defined by a federation scheme that in turn defines a federation distribution key, which determines the distribution of data across the federated database partitions. Essentially, it is a horizontal partition of your database. For example, in a 100-row database, rows 1 through 50 can be in one partition and rows 51 to 100 can be in another partition. A federation is used to achieve greater scalability and performance from the database portion of your application.

Each database partition within a federation is known as a federation member and has its own schema; it contains the federated table rows that correspond to its range. For example, in our earlier example, the federated table will contain rows 1 to 50 for the federated member containing the range 1 to 50. Federated tables are tables that are spread across federation members. Each member can also contain reference tables, which are not federation aware. In other words, the reference table is wholly contained within a member and usually contains information that is referenced in relation to the federated table within that member.

Federations are accessed through a federation root database. The root performs the routing to the appropriate federation members based on the given federation key value. Each root may contain multiple federations, each with its own federation scheme. The root database in Figure 3-4 points to two federations, each with two databases partitions, or federation members.

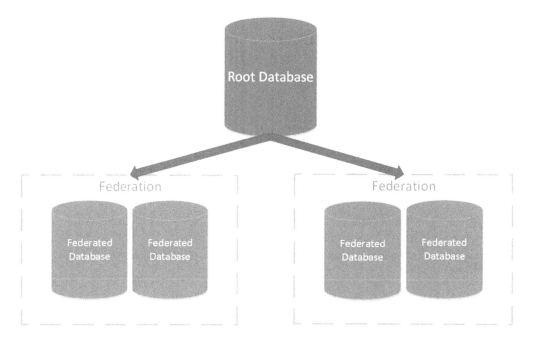

Figure 3-4. *A federation root database points to multiple federations. Each federation contains the federated databases*

Geospatial Representation in SQL Database

Microsoft has had support for geospatial types since SQL Server 2008. By extension, SQL Database can represent and store geospatial data. Before we describe how geospatial data is represented in SQL Database, we will give you an overview of spatial reference systems.

Spatial Reference Systems Overview

A spatial reference system (SRS) is a system to represent a point on the Earth uniquely. There are, in fact, many spatial reference systems, so it follows that there are many ways a point on the Earth can be represented. An SRS must be able to specify types of coordinates used (such as latitude/longitude or easting/northing coordinates), from where those coordinates are measured, the units of the coordinates, and the shape of the Earth over which those coordinates extend.

The Earth is not a simple sphere, but rather is a complex shape. Its shape is called a *geoid* and it represents the Earth, and only the Earth. Because it is such a complicated shape to represent, it is approximated using different ellipsoids. Each approximation affects the accuracy at different positions on the planet. Once the correct model ellipsoid is chosen, it must also be aligned with the Earth by using a frame of reference. There are, again, various frames of references defined. Together, the reference ellipsoid and the reference frame form a *geodetic datum*, of which the most-known one is the World Geodetic System of 1984 (WGS84).

Latitudes and longitudes are two of the more common ways of representing a point in space; it can be represented as a decimal (37.775192,-122.419381) or in degrees, minutes, and seconds (37° 46' 30.6906", -122° 25' 9.768"). The next challenge is to represent a 3D world on a 2D plane. That is where projection becomes important. Once again, there are different methods of projecting the Earth onto a 2D plane, of which the most common is the *Mercator Projection*. Both Bing and Google Maps use the Mercator projection.

SQL Database Spatial Data Types

Now that you have a slightly better idea of spatial references, we can show you how SQL Database supports this data. There are two types of spatial data supported by SQL Database: geometry and geography. The geometry data type supports planar or (flat-Earth) data. The geography data type supports ellipsoidal (round-Earth) data. Both the geometry and geography data types support various spatial data objects, as depicted in Figure 3-5. The data objects can be categorized as follows:

- **Single geometries**: contain only one discrete geometric element. The single geometries represented by SQL Database are points (`Point`), curves (`LineString`, `CircularString`, and `Compound String`), and surfaces (`Polygon` and `CurvePolygon`).

- **Geometry collections**: contain one or more of the single geometries. There are two types of geometry collections: homogeneous and heterogeneous. A homogeneous collection contains only one type of single geometry, and a heterogeneous collection contains one or more of the single geometries.

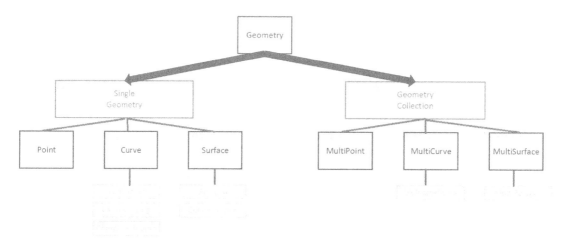

Figure 3-5. *SQL Database geometries are the same as SQL Server geometries*

Figure 3-5 depicts the different types of geometries that are supported by SQL Database.

While both geometry and geography data types support the same geometries, they differ in the way they represent the types. For example, both geometry and geography data types can represent an edge between two verities; however, in the geometry type the edge is a straight line, and in the geography type the edge is an elliptic arc.

SQL Database also provides methods for manipulating the spatial data types. There are methods for constructing geometry from Well-Known Text (WKT) Input:

- STGeomFromText: constructs any type of geometry instance from WKT input

- STPointFromText: constructs a geometry Point from WKT

- STMPointFromText: constructs a geometry MultiPoint from WKT

- STLineFromText: constructs a geometry LineString from WKT

- STMLineFromText: constructs a geometry MultiLineString from WKT

- STPolyFromText: constructs a geometry Polygon from WKT

- STMPolyFromText: constructs a geometry MultiPolygon from WKT

- STGeomColFromText: constructs a geometry GeometryCollection from WKT

There are also methods for constructing geometry from Well-Known Binary (WKB) Input, which have the same functionality as the previous methods other than the input: STGeomFromWKB, STPointFromWKB, STMPointFromWKB, STLineFromWKB, STMLineFromWKB, STPolyFromWKB, STMPolyFromWKB, and STGeomColFromWKB.

An example of how to call one of these static methods is:

```
DECLARE @g geometry;
SET @g = geometry::STPointFromText('POINT (100 100)', 0);
SELECT @g.ToString();
```

In the sample application that follows, we will be using this very spatial type in order to represent a latitude and a longitude.

Setting Up a SQL Database

In this section, we will describe how to set up a SQL Database. Much of the database can be set up and managed through the management portal. Alternatively, many tasks can be handled programmatically. For example, you may choose to create tables through the management portal associated with your Azure account, or you may create tables in your code. We will show you how to do both in this chapter. Complete the following steps to create a SQL Database:

1. Log on to your management portal on www.windowsazure.com. As always, you will need your Windows Live ID to log in.

2. Click on SQL Databases on the left-hand menu. If this is your first time, then you should have no SQL Databases in the portal, as is the case in Figure 3-6. You can click CREATE A SQL DATABASE to create your first database.

Figure 3-6. *There are no SQL Databases associated with this account. To create one, you click on CREATE A SQL DATABASE*

3. You should name the database and choose a server. In Figure 3-7, we have named the database EarthquakeMap and selected a new SQL Database server. As explained earlier, once you complete the creation process, Azure will provide a server name for you in the provisioning process.

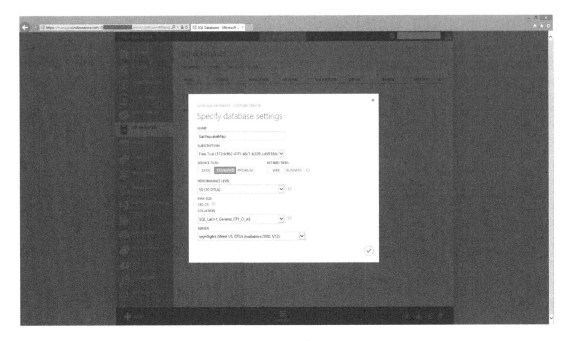

Figure 3-7. *You can select a name and type of server for your new database*

4. You will be asked to select a login name and password. Jot down what you've chosen, as you will be required to have the login information for interacting with the database.

5. Once you are done entering the server settings (login and password), click on the check mark if you are satisfied with your choices, and you will have created your database! Your management portal will now list this database and server, as in Figure 3-8.

Figure 3-8. *The management portal lists the databases and servers associated with your account*

6. You now have to configure the firewall settings. You must add your IP to the list of allowable addresses by clicking on the database and then clicking on "Manage allowed IP addresses."

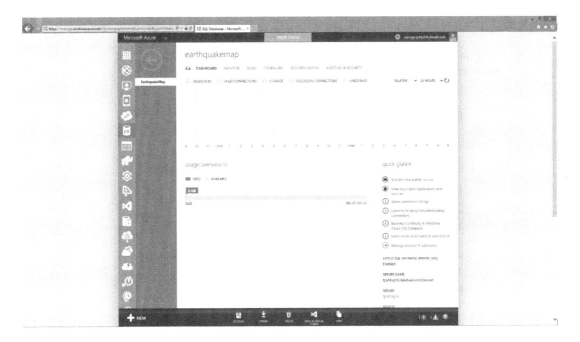

Figure 3-9. *Manage the database created from this portal, such as adding IP addresses to whitelist*

CHAPTER 3 ▪ GEOSPATIAL DATA WITH AZURE SQL DATABASE

7. Click on ADD TO THE ALLOWED IP ADDRESSES to add the current client IP addresses to the whitelist. In Figure 3-10 there are three IP addresses that are allowed.

Figure 3-10. *Manage allowed IP addresses*

8. Go back to the SQL portalDatabase page by clicking the DB icon: .

9. Click on the white arrow listed by your database name to return to the management portal for the database, as shown in Figure 3-11.

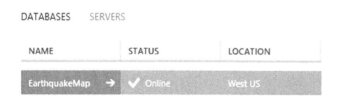

Figure 3-11. *The created database as listed by the SQL Database management portal*

10. The management portal for that database will appear, as in Figure 3-12.

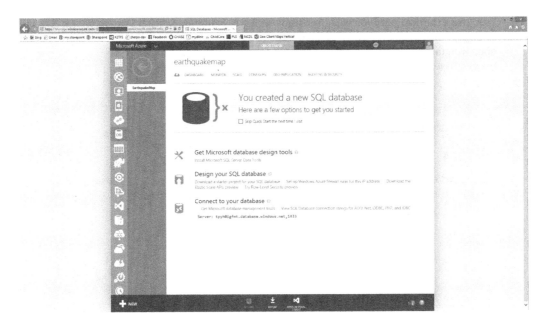

Figure 3-12. *The management portal for the newly created database*

■ **Note**   On the links near quick glance, there is the option to preview the new portal. Clicking on "Visit the new portal" will bring you to the portal. The portal appears as in Figure 3-13.

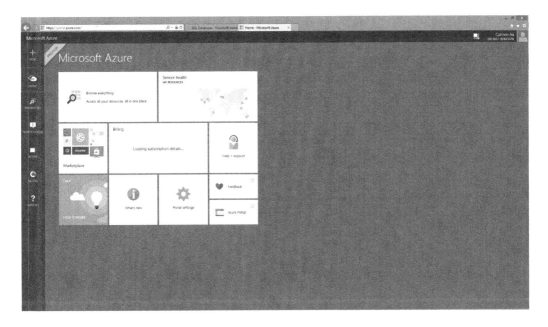

Figure 3-13. *Preview of the new Azure portal*

11. To manage the database, you will do go into the Server Explorer of Visual Studio. Click on "Open in Visual Studio" at the bottom of the screen. Visual Studio will open with the SQL Server Object Explorer window open. You will be able to see the database, EarthquakeMap, that you created. See Figure 3-14.

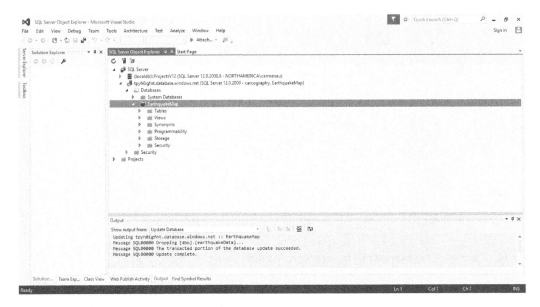

Figure 3-14. *SQL Server Object Explorer in Visual Studio 2015*

12. To start a query, right-click on your database and select New Query as in Figure 3-15.

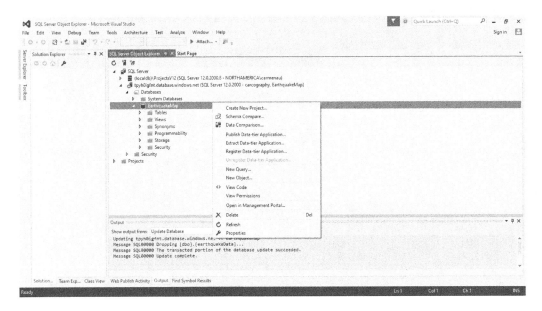

Figure 3-15. *Select New Query from the context menu to start a new query on your database*

13.   Enter the query and hit Run. In the following code listing, we show you an example of how you can create a new table for the newly created database:

```
-- Create the earthquakeData table.
    IF NOT EXISTS (SELECT * FROM sys.objects
        WHERE object_id = OBJECT_ID(N'[dbo].[EarthquakeData]')
        AND type in (N'U'))
    BEGIN
    CREATE TABLE [dbo].[EarthquakeData](
        [DateTime] [datetime] NOT NULL,
        [Position] [Geography] NOT NULL,
        [Depth] [float] NOT NULL,
        [Magnitude] [float] NOT NULL,
        [MagType] [nvarchar](50) NOT NULL,
        [NbStation] [int] NOT NULL,
        [Gap] [int] NOT NULL,
        [Distance] [float] NOT NULL,
        [RMS] [float] NOT NULL,
        [EventID] [nvarchar](50) NOT NULL,
        [Source] [float] NOT NULL,
        )
    END;
    GO
```

14.   After running the query, you now have a server that has one database that has one table; see Figure 3-16.

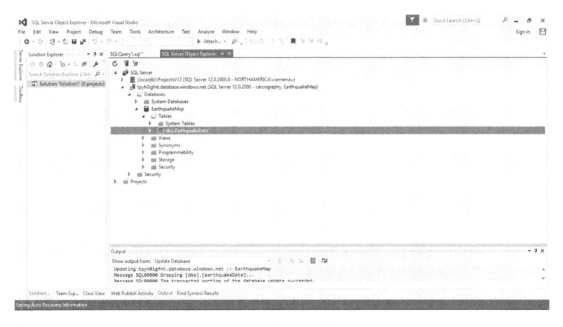

Figure 3-16. *Your database now contains one table, EarthquakeData*

Inserting Geospatial Data into a SQL Database

In this section, we will be showing you how to insert data into your SQL Database. In our book example, we are creating an application that displays earthquake data. You can retrieve the daily updates of all the earthquakes that occurred in the previous 2.5 days at the following website: `http://on.doi.gov/1CySGBT`. In Figure 3-17, you can see a sample CSV (Comma Separated Values) ile containing the earthquake data.

	A	B	C	D	E	F	G	H	I	J	K	L	M	N	O	P
1	time	latitude	longitude	depth	mag	magType	nst	gap	dmin	rms	net	id	updated	place	type	
2	2015-06-28T15:54:42.940Z	16.7413	-94.5177	100.59	5.1	mb			129	2.329	0.95	us	us10002m	2015-06-2	22km NNE	earthquake	
3	2015-06-28T15:21:51.110Z	39.2593	72.3655	10	4.4	mb			78	0.489	1.02	us	us10002m	2015-06-2	72km E of	earthquake	
4	2015-06-28T15:21:12.570Z	82.6319	118.9978	10	4.4	mb			111	15.081	0.66	us	us10002m	2015-06-2	North of S	earthquake	
5	2015-06-28T14:44:19.200Z	-18.158	-178.4198	623.29	4.4	mb			86	3.382	0.91	us	us10002m	2015-06-2	277km N	earthquake	
6	2015-06-28T14:37:15.290Z	36.293	-97.5156	5	3.4	mb_lg			85	0.432	0.28	us	us10002m	2015-06-2	20km W o	earthquake	
7	2015-06-28T14:03:04.390Z	42.7406	139.0395	218.8	4.1	mb			45	1.774	0.7	us	us10002m	2015-06-2	122km WS	earthquake	
8	2015-06-28T12:53:49.940Z	-32.2164	-178.0186	10	5.2	mb			74	2.962	1.31	us	us10002m	2015-06-2	120km SE	earthquake	
9	2015-06-28T12:36:30.000Z	60.6421	-151.9833	79.1	3.4	ml					0.84	ak	ak116363	2015-06-2	38km W o	earthquake	
10	2015-06-28T09:15:03.350Z	47.391	-70.0837	9.52	3.3	mb_lg			180	0.769	0.33	us	us10002m	2015-06-2	5km NNW	earthquake	
11	2015-06-28T08:54:47.550Z	19.3008327	-155.2061615	8.01	3.11	ml	61		121	0.02617	0.27	hv	hv609683	2015-06-2	14km SSE	earthquake	
12	2015-06-28T08:54:47.480Z	19.3125	-155.2041667	8.88	3.2	ml	52		102	0.03663	0.09	hv	hv609683	2015-06-2	13km SSE	earthquake	
13	2015-06-28T08:10:10.480Z	19.335	-155.2093333	8.55	5.2	ml	63		74	0.03902	0.09	hv	hv609682	2015-06-2	13km S of	earthquake	
14	2015-06-28T02:09:18.000Z	63.3236	-150.5339	139.1	3.1	ml					0.37	ak	ak116359	2015-06-2	79km W o	earthquake	
15	2015-06-28T01:35:19.850Z	36.6565	-98.1488	5	3.6	mb_lg			91	0.155	0.75	us	us10002m	2015-06-2	16km NE	earthquake	
16	2015-06-28T01:05:28.640Z	26.6165	90.4387	26	5.5	mb			36	1.648	1.05	us	us10002m	2015-06-2	17km NNE	earthquake	
17	2015-06-28T01:04:38.920Z	36.4536	-98.116	5	2.7	mb_lg			89	0.118	0.67	us	us10002m	2015-06-2	17km SE o	earthquake	
18	2015-06-28T00:44:23.000Z	56.462	-156.3767	97	2.7	ml					0.97	ak	ak116359	2015-06-2	85km W o	earthquake	
19	2015-06-28T00:18:00.310Z	35.7717	-97.3875	4.14	3.1	mb_lg			37	0.06	0.66	us	us10002m	2015-06-2	12km SSE	earthquake	
20	2015-06-27T23:48:43.640Z	-17.9193	65.3481	10	4.9	mb			73	12.53	0.65	us	us10002m	2015-06-2	282km NE	earthquake	
21	2015-06-27T23:45:11.910Z	41.123333	-123.5053329	37.91	2.87	ml	34		47	0.1602	0.21	nc	nc724732	2015-06-2	22km NNE	earthquake	
22	2015-06-27T23:29:33.210Z	-31.2667	-177.6172	10	4.7	mb			186	2.033	1.08	us	us10002m	2015-06-2	123km E o	earthquake	
23	2015-06-27T22:49:07.010Z	36.5785	-97.5627	1.3	3.1	mb_lg			40	0.333	0.49	us	us10002m	2015-06-2	25km WS\	earthquake	
24	2015-06-27T22:42:12.710Z	-5.9831	147.1779	56.45	4.5	mb			79	3.918	0.75	us	us10002m	2015-06-2	84km NNE	earthquake	
25	2015-06-27T22:19:27.000Z	58.7239	-142.281	0	2.7	ml					1.04	ak	ak116358	2015-06-2	149km S o	earthquake	
26	2015-06-27T21:53:54.810Z	3.7866	122.41	596.88	4.4	mb			77	3.115	0.62	us	us10002m	2015-06-2	254km SE	earthquake	
27	2015-06-27T21:30:08.600Z	-5.4286	152.2692	35	4.9	mb			95	1.233	1.34	us	us10002m	2015-06-2	119km S o	earthquake	
28																

Figure 3-17. *Sample earthquake data from* `http://earthquake.usgs.gov/earthquakes/feed/v1.0/summary/2.5_day.csv`

1. Start a new Microsoft Visual Studio 2015 Console Application project. We have named our project `ReadGeospatialDataToSQL`.

2. You will now need a class to hold all of the earthquake data. We create the class `Earthquake.cs`, which appears as follows:

```
using System;
using Microsoft.Maps.MapControl.WPF;

namespace ReadGeospatialDataToSql
{
    public class Earthquake
    {
        public DateTime When { get; set; }
        public Location Location { get; set; }
        public float Depth { get; set; }
        public float Magnitude { get; set; }
        public string MagType { get; set; }
        public int NbStation { get; set; }
        public float Gap { get; set; }
        public float Distance { get; set; }
```

```
public float RMS { get; set; }
public string Source { get; set; }
public string EventID { get; set; }
public string Title { get; set; }
public string Description { get; set; }

public Earthquake(DateTime when, Location where, float depth, float
magnitude, string magType,
    int nbStation, float gap, float distance, float rms, string source,
    string eventId, string title, string description = "")

{
    When = when;
    Location = where;
    Depth = depth;
    Magnitude = magnitude;
    MagType = magType;
    NbStation = nbStation;
    Gap = gap;
    Distance = distance;
    RMS = rms;
    Source = source;
    EventID = eventId;
    Title = title;
    Description = description;
}
    }
}
```

■ **Note**   You will need to add `Microsoft.Maps.Control.WPF.dll` as a reference to this project. If you did not already download the Bing Maps Window Presentation Foundation (WPF) Control, you can do so here: `http://bit.ly/16xHcy1`. Depending on where you installed the SDK, you will be able to find it here: `<Bing Maps WPF Control Location>\V1\Libraries`. For example, ours was here: `C:\Program Files (x86)\Bing Maps WPF Control\V1\Libraries`.

3. Additionally, you will require a CSV file reader, `CSVFileReader.cs`. You can find one at `http://bit.ly/1Ho8Jz6`. We have refactored the code to only contain the reader, as we do not need a CSV writer for this sample.

4. Now, you are ready to write the code to read the CSV earthquake data file into the Earthquake object: `private static List<Earthquake> _data = new List<Earthquake>();` which is a member of the class containing the `GetRecentEarthquakes()` method:

```
public static void GetRecentEarthquakes()
{

    WebClient client = new WebClient();
    Uri quakeDataURL = new Uri("http://earthquake.usgs.gov/earthquakes/feed/v1.0/
    summary/2.5_day.csv");
```

```csharp
string quakeDataFile = "quake.csv";
client.DownloadFile(quakeDataURL, quakeDataFile);
CSVFileReader reader = new CSVFileReader(quakeDataFile);
List<string> columns = new List<String>();
bool readHeader = false;
while (reader.ReadRow(columns))
{
    Debug.Assert(true);
    if (readHeader)
    {

        DateTime when = DateTime.Parse(columns[0]);
        double lat = Convert.ToDouble(columns[1]);
        double lon = Convert.ToDouble(columns[2]);
        Location where = new Location(lat, lon);
        float depth = columns[3] != "" ? Convert.ToSingle(columns[3]) : 0.0f;
        float magnitude = columns[4] != "" ? Convert.ToSingle(columns[4]) :
        0.0f;
        string magType = columns[5];
        int nbStation = columns[6] != "" ? Convert.ToInt16(columns[6]) : 0;
        float gap = columns[7] != "" ? Convert.ToSingle(columns[7]) : 0;
        float distance = columns[8] != "" ? Convert.ToSingle(columns[8]) :
        0.0f;
        float rms = columns[9] != "" ? Convert.ToSingle(columns[9]) : 0.0f;
        string source = columns[10];
        string eventId = columns[11];
        _data.Add(new Earthquake(when,
                                 where,
                                 depth,
                                 magnitude,
                                 magType,
                                 nbStation,
                                 gap,
                                 distance,
                                 rms,
                                 source,
                                 eventId,
                                 "M " + columns[4]));

    }
    else
    {
        readHeader = true;
    }
}
}
```

5. Finally, you can write the code to read the earthquake data into the SQL database. We will show you how to create the table programmatically. The SQL server login and password you created earlier will be useful. The username is a combination of the login and the server in the format <loginname>@<servername>; for example, if your login is myLogin and your server is myServername then your username will be myLogin@myServername.

It is good to note that the DateTime field is inserted into the SQL Database using a parameter @value. This abstraction is necessary due to the fact that DateTime types require single quotes around them to be inserted–for example, '20130107'–however, it can be often confused with a string, hence the need for the parameter.

Another interesting type is the geometry type, which is one of the geospatial types supported by SQL Database, as we described earlier. . Here, we used a single geometry, Point, to represent our latitude and longitude:

```
public static void insertQuakeDataToSQL()
    {
        // Provide the following information
        string userName = myLogin@myServername;
        string password = myPassword;
        string dataSource = "myServername.database.windows.net";
        string sampleDatabaseName = "EarthquakeMap";

        // Create a connection string for the sample database
        SqlConnectionStringBuilder connString2Builder;
        connString2Builder = new SqlConnectionStringBuilder();
        connString2Builder.DataSource = dataSource;
        connString2Builder.InitialCatalog = sampleDatabaseName;
        connString2Builder.Encrypt = true;
        connString2Builder.TrustServerCertificate = false;
        connString2Builder.UserID = userName;
        connString2Builder.Password = password;

        // Connect to the sample database and perform various operations
        var mystring = connString2Builder.ToString();
        Console.WriteLine(mystring);
        using (SqlConnection conn = new SqlConnection(connString2Builder.ToString()))
        {
            string tableName = "earthquakeData";

            SqlCommand cmd = conn.CreateCommand();
            conn.Open();
            // Create a table
            cmd.CommandText = "CREATE TABLE " + tableName + "(" +
                            "DateTime datetime primary key," +
                            "Position geography," +
                            "Depth float," +
                            "Magnitude float," +
                            "MagType varchar(20)," +
                            "NbStation int," +
                            "Gap float," +
                            "Distance float," +
                            "RMS float," +
```

```
                                "Source varchar(20)," +
                                "EventID varchar(20)," +
                                "Title varchar(20)," +
                                "Description varchar(30))";
            cmd.ExecuteNonQuery();

            // delete data from table
            cmd.CommandText = "DELETE FROM " + tableName;
            cmd.ExecuteNonQuery();

            string columnsToInsert = "INSERT INTO " + tableName + "(" +
                                "DateTime," +
                                "Position," +
                                "Depth," +
                                "Magnitude," +
                                "MagType," +
                                "NbStation," +
                                "Gap," +
                                "Distance," +
                                "RMS," +
                                "Source," +
                                "EventID," +
                                "Title)";
            // INSERT data into SQL database
            foreach (var line in _data)
            {
                cmd = conn.CreateCommand();
                string valuesToInsert = " VALUES (" +
                                "@value," +
                                "geography::Point(" + line.Location.Latitude + ","
                                + line.Location.Longitude +
                                ", 4326), " +
                                line.Depth + "," +
                                line.Magnitude + ",'" +
                                line.MagType + "'," +
                                line.NbStation + ", " +
                                line.Gap + ", " +
                                line.Distance + ", " +
                                line.RMS + ", '" +
                                line.Source + "', '" +
                                line.EventID + "', '" +
                                line.Title + "')";
                string commandString = columnsToInsert + valuesToInsert;
                cmd.CommandText = commandString;
                cmd.Parameters.AddWithValue("@value", line.When);
                cmd.ExecuteNonQuery();
                cmd.Dispose();
            }

    // View the data from the table
            cmd.CommandText = "SELECT * FROM " + tableName;
            using (SqlDataReader reader = cmd.ExecuteReader())
```

```
    {
        while (reader.Read())
        {
            Console.WriteLine("{0}, {1}, {2}", reader["DateTime"].ToString().
            Trim(),
                               reader["Position"].ToString().Trim(),
                               reader["Magnitude"].ToString().Trim());
        }
    }
    conn.Close();
    }
}
```

▪ **Note**   Once you have created the table, you no longer have to create this table each time you run this code. So, you can either remove that part of the code, or you can always use the DELETE FROM <table> SQL command.

Wrapping Up

In this chapter, you learned about hosting geospatial data on SQL Database. As you probably noted, transitioning from SQL Server to SQL Database is straightforward. One nice difference is the availability of the management portal. On the portal, you can create, manage, and delete databases. Of course, as an alternative to the management portal, you can still do many of the tasks, such as creating tables, programmatically rather than on the portal.

In our sample code in this chapter, we pulled geospatial data from the government earthquake site http://on.doi.gov/1cXCj1C. We inserted the code into an Earthquake class and then inserted this data into our SQL database that we created in this chapter. In the following chapter, you will learn about WCF and how we can use it to provide a service that queries the database for client applications.

CHAPTER 4

■ ■ ■

Hosting WCF Services on Microsoft Azure

In Chapter 3, we showed you how to import your geospatial data into an Azure SQL Database. In this chapter, we will show you how to create and host WCF (Windows Communication Foundation) Services on Microsoft Azure that will serve your geospatial data to a client application. In the following section, we will give you a quick crash course about WCF. For a deeper understanding of it, we recommend a dedicated WCF book, such as *Pro WCF4: Practical Microsoft SOA Implementation* by Nishith Pathak.

WCF: A Crash Course

WCF is a framework for developing and deploying service-oriented applications. These services are loosely coupled, provide some functionality, and have no internal calls to one another. Using WCF, data can be sent asynchronously between service endpoints. Together, a group of services will provide the complete functionality of an entire software application. For example, if building an ATM machine software, one service could handle the login, another display the balance, and another count and subtract. These services provide the total functionality for the ATM machine software. This type of service-oriented design principle is known as service-oriented architecture (SOA), which is the architecture on which WCF is built. We will now describe the services and how they communicate.

Services

SOA allows for distributed computing such that services need not be co-located. Moreover, services can have multiple parties using them and can execute on different timelines. Services can even be version independent.

Clients consume the functionality of the service. Examples of clients can be WPF, a Windows form, or even an ASP.NET webpage. The client and service communicate by sending messages back and forth. The service exposes metadata describing the functionality of the service and also how clients should communicate with it. The client then communicates indirectly with the service using a proxy. A client's proxy can communicate with one or more services' endpoints. As you can see in Figure 4-1, there are two locations; perhaps "Location 1" is local and "Location 2" is remote. Machine 2 is running a client and can communicate with the service that is running on Machine 1 via the client proxy. Likewise, Machine 4 has a client whose proxy is communicating with the service running on Machine 3. Additionally, Machine 4's client is also communicating with Machine 1's service via the Internet. In the example in Figure 4-1, we see that a client can communicate with a service remotely, but also that it can communicate with more than one service. Since the client uses proxies, the programming model is simplified, as all types of clients, regardless of location, require the use of a proxy.

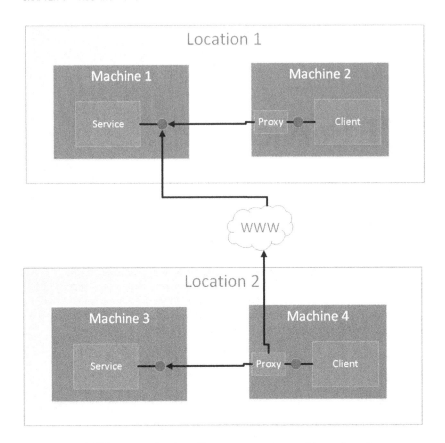

Figure 4-1. *WCF communication: clients communicate with services via a proxy*

In Figure 4-1, there are also purple circles that represent endpoints. The endpoints contain addresses, bindings, and contracts, which conveniently can be abbreviated to ABC. We will describe the ABCs of endpoints subsequently.

Endpoints

The endpoint comprises the fusion of three parts: addresses, bindings, and contracts, as shown in Figure 4-2. Each endpoint must contain all three parts. Every service must expose at least one endpoint; however, it can have multiple endpoints. These endpoints can use the same or different bindings and can have the same or different contracts. There is no relationship between these endpoints.

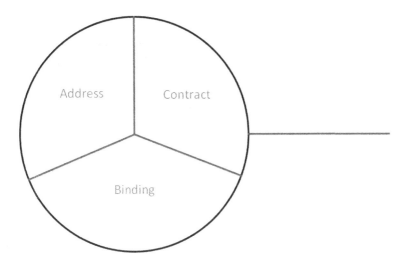

Figure 4-2. Endpoints

Addresses

In WCF, every service has a unique address with the following format: [base address]/[optional URI], where the base address looks like: [transport scheme]://[machine or domain][:optional port].

- A transport scheme is any one of the following supported schemes:

  - HTTP/HTTPS

  - TCP

  - IPC

  - Peer network

  - MSMQ

  - Service bus

An example service address would be *http://localhost:8000* or *net.tcp//localhost:8002/myservice*.

Bindings

The binding is what specifies how the data will be transferred by specifying the communication protocol. The first aspect of data transfer to consider is the method of transport. Earlier, we listed some of the supported transport protocols (HTTP, TCP, etc.). In addition to the different transport protocols, there are different options for encoding that message. For example, you can choose to leave the message as plain text, or you can use a binary encoding, or, for larger payloads, you can use Message Transport Optimization Mechanism (MTOM). There are also different options for message authentication from which to choose. As the message delivery may not always be reliable, it is important that the message be authenticated. Other choices are the type of security, the transaction propagation, and the interoperability. As you can see, there are potentially tens of thousands of permutations you can choose from simply to transfer your messages. WCF simplifies your choices by grouping together sets of communications that include your transport protocol, your message encoding, and your message authentication into pre-defined bindings. The binding, therefore, is a consistent, pre-defined set of choices for your message communication.

Here are some common bindings:

- **Basic binding**: basically looks like a legacy web service that communicates over the basic web-service profile.

- **TCP binding**: uses TCP for communication over the intranet

- **IPC binding**: for same-machine communication

- **Web-service binding**: uses HTTP or HTTPS for transport over the Internet

- **MSMQ binding**: used for disconnected queued calls

Which binding you choose is largely an architectural decision. For example, a web service supporting external clients running in web browsers would likely choose the web-service binding; a dedicated client server running in C# might use TCP binding because it's lower overhead, or web-service binding to permit other web clients to have access over the lifespan of the application. When in doubt, the web-service binding is a logical choice.

Contracts

Services expose *contracts* that describe what the service does via an *endpoint*. There are different types of contracts defined by WCF:

- **Service contracts**: describe what operations can be performed by the client on the service

- **Data contracts**: describe what type of data are passed to and from the service. While int and string are the two pre-defined types, you can also define some custom types.

- **Fault contracts**: define which errors are raised by the service and how the service handles those errors

- **Message contracts**: allow the service to interact directly with the message

An example of an endpoint can be as follows:

```
<system.serviceModel>
  <services>
    <service name = "MyNamespace.MyService">
      <endpoint
        address = "http://localhost:8000/MyService"
        binding = "wsHttpBinding"
        contract = "MyNamespace.IMyContract"
      />
    </service>
  </services>
</system.serviceModel>
```

You can have multiple endpoints for the same service, and that will look as follows:

```
<system.serviceModel>
  <services>
    <service name = "MyNamespace.MyService">
      <endpoint
        address = "http://localhost:8000/MyService"
        binding = "wsHttpBinding"
        contract = "MyNamespace.IMyContract"
      />
      <endpoint
        address = "net.tcp://localhost:8002/MyService"
        binding = "NetTcpBinding"
        contract = "MyNamespace.IMyContract"
      />
      <endpoint
        address = "net.msmq://localhost/private/MyQueue"
        binding = "NetMsmqBinding"
        contract = "MyNamespace.IMyOtherContract"
      />
    </service>
  </services>
</system.serviceModel>
```

Alternatively, you can just rely on WCF to add the default endpoints to the services and not provide the endpoint specifications. For example, if using HTTP, WCF will use the basic binding.

Hosting

One additional aspect to discuss is the concept of hosting. Every WCF service is hosted in a Windows process called the host process, which can host multiple services. Moreover, a single service can be hosted by multiple processes. The host can be provided by Internet Information Services (IIS), Windows Activation Service (WAS), or, more recently, by Windows Server AppFabric. The host can also be provided by the developer as part of the application. Windows Server AppFabric provides additional configuration options, monitoring, instrumentation, and event tracking for both WCF services and Workflow services. It allows the services to auto-start without requiring the first client request. A service host will look as follows:

```
ServiceHost host = new ServiceHost(typeof(MyService),
  httpBaseAddress,
  tcpBaseAddress,
  icpBaseAddress);
host.Open();
```

WCF Client

A WCF client application uses the WCF client proxy to communicate with the service. The application imports the service's metadata to generate the necessary code that can be used to invoke the service. The client first must compile the service code, then it must generate the WCF client proxy, and finally it must instantiate the WCF client proxy, after which the client is able to use the service.

WCF Client Proxy

The client proxy can be generated using Visual Studio by using the Add Service Reference option (right-click the project in the Solution Explorer). Alternatively, it can be generated by using the Service Model Metadata Utility Tool, which is a command-line tool for generating code from metadata.

WCF Service for Earthquake Data

In this section, we will show you how to build a WCF service that enables a client application to query the database for the earthquake data we loaded into Azure SQL Database in Chapter 3. We will then show you how you can host this service on Azure and, finally, how to write a client application that calls the service.

Creating the WCF Service

1. As an administrator, run Visual Studio 2015. To run as administrator, you will right-click the application and select Run as Administrator.

2. In the menu, start a new project by selecting File ➤ New ➤ Project.

3. Under Templates, select Visual C# and then Cloud, and select Azure Cloud Service. We named our project WCFEarthquakeService. Click OK. See Figure 4-3.

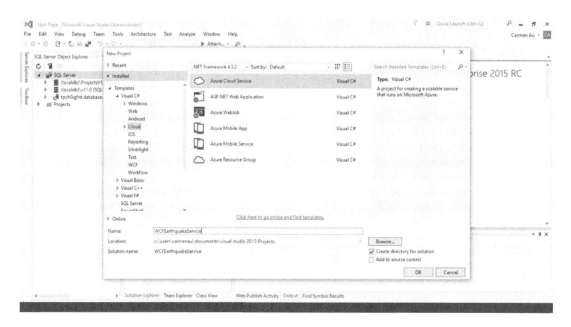

Figure 4-3. *Create an Azure Cloud Service in Visual Studio 2015*

4. In the resulting New Microsoft Azure Cloud Service window, select from the Visual C# .NET Framework roles the WCF Service Web Role, and click > to add the role to the Microsoft Azure Cloud Service solution. Click OK. Visual Studio will create the solution. See Figure 4-4.

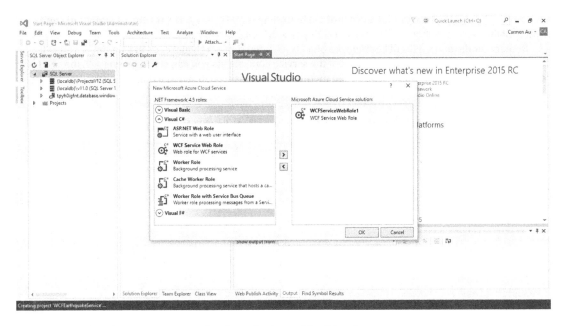

Figure 4-4. *Select the WCF Service Web Role as the Azure Cloud Service*

5. Select IService.cs in order to modify it to your service with the desired interface. In our case, you will add the following code listing:

Listing 4-1. IService.cs service interface for the WCF service

```
using System.Collections.Generic;
using System.ServiceModel;

namespace WCFServiceWebRole1
{
    [ServiceContract]
    public interface IService1
    {

        [OperationContract]
        List<Earthquake> GetEarthquakeData();

        [OperationContract]
        List<Earthquake> GetEarthquakeDataBBox(double TLLong, double TLLat,
            double BRLong, double BRLat);
    }
}
```

You will note that in Listing 4-1 there are two methods declared; each method has the declaration [OperationContract] that precedes it to indicate that the method defines an operation that is part of a service contract for a WCF application. Both methods will retrieve earthquake data from the Azure SQL Database–the first will return all earthquake data in the database, and the second, GetEarthquakeDataBBox, will return the earthquake data that is within a given bounding box. The bounding box is defined by the

61

longitude and latitude of the top-left corner of the bounding box (TLLong, TLLat) and the longitude and latitude of the bottom-right corner of the bounding box (BRLong and BRLat).

Both methods return a list of Earthquake objects as defined in Earthquake.cs in Chapter 3. You will need to modify this class in order to be part of the service contract. As you can see in Listing 4-2, the class is defined as part of the data contract, and each member of the class is defined as a data member.

■ **Note** Don't forget to add the MapControl reference in order to be able to use the Location type.

Listing 4-2. Earthquake.cs. Each member must be explicitly defined as a data member

```
using System;
using System.Runtime.Serialization;
using Microsoft.Maps.MapControl.WPF;

namespace WCFServiceWebRole1
{
    [DataContract]
    public class Earthquake
    {
        [DataMember]
        public DateTime When { get; set; }
        [DataMember]
        public Location Location { get; set; }
        [DataMember]
        public float Depth { get; set; }
        [DataMember]
        public float Magnitude { get; set; }
        [DataMember]
        public string MagType { get; set; }
        [DataMember]
        public int NbStation { get; set; }
        [DataMember]
        public float Gap { get; set; }
        [DataMember]
        public float Distance { get; set; }
        [DataMember]
        public float RMS { get; set; }
        [DataMember]
        public string Source { get; set; }
        [DataMember]
        public string EventID { get; set; }
        [DataMember]
        public string Title { get; set; }
        [DataMember]
        public string Description { get; set; }
```

```
        public Earthquake()
        {

        }

        public Earthquake(DateTime when, Location where, float depth, float magnitude,
        string magType,
            int nbStation, float gap, float distance, float rms, string source, string eventId,
            string title, string description = "")
        {
            When = when;
            Location = where;
            Depth = depth;
            Magnitude = magnitude;
            MagType = magType;
            NbStation = nbStation;
            Gap = gap;
            Distance = distance;
            RMS = rms;
            Source = source;
            EventID = eventId;
            Title = title;
            Description = description;
        }
    }
}
```

6. Next, we will modify the Service1.svc.cs, which contains the implementation of the two methods declared in the service interface, IService.cs. To implement GetEarthquakeData(), you will query the database for all the earthquakes with the following query string:

```
SELECT <desired fields> FROM <my SQL table name>.
```

In our case it will be:

```
SELECT DateTime, Position, Magnitude, Depth, MagType, NbStation, Gap, Distance, RMS, Source,
EventID, Version, Title FROM earthquakeData
```

The full listing for this method is seen in Listing 4-3.

Listing 4-3. Method to create query string to request all earthquakes from the SQL database

```
public List<Earthquake> GetEarthquakeData()
        {
            string tableName = "earthquakeData";
            var queryString = "SELECT DateTime, " +
                              "Position, " +
                              "Magnitude, " +
                              "Depth, " +
                              "MagType, " +
```

```
                        "NbStation, " +
                        "Gap, " +
                        "Distance, " +
                        "RMS, " +
                        "Source, " +
                        "EventID, " +
                        "Title FROM " + tableName;
        return GetEarthquakesFromSql(queryString);
    }
```

Clearly, there is an important part of the code that has been abstracted away, which you will find in the method GetEarthquakesFromSql. First, you will create the connection to the database as you did in Chapter 3. You will use the same credentials as you did in Chapter 3, and you should also be using the same server, database, and table as in Chapter 3, if you want to retrieve the same earthquake data you fetched in the earlier example.

Once you have retrieved the data, you will need to parse this data into the Earthquake class and append it to the list of Earthquakes we have defined as data. For the most part, parsing the data is straightforward, particularly when retrieving common types such as string and int. You must simply cast the SQL objects to the correct types. You will note the odd double cast for magnitude and other data that was stored as float types in SQL. For some reason, a float in SQL Server is retrieved to .NET type double, so you will need to cast to double and then cast back to float. Lastly, we look at how to parse the geography data. When the SQL reader receives the geography data from the SQL database, the type of this data is not yet known to the reader. Thus, a direct cast is not possible. The workaround for this issue is to read the data into a byte array and then cast to the SQLGeography type. From there, you can convert this data into the Location type from the MapControl that the Earthquake object expects for Location data.

In order to use the SQLGeography type, you will need to include a reference to the SqlServer.Types. You can usually find this library where you have your SQL Server libraries on your machine. In our case it was in the following:

```
C:\Program Files (x86)\Microsoft SQL Server\120\SDK\Assemblies
```

■ **Note** In order for the references to be included in the package you will be creating for Azure, right-click on the reference and select Properties. Under Copy Local, you should make sure it is True; leaving the property to be False will result in the reference not being copied to the output directory, and therefore it will not be included in the service package you deploy to Azure.

The namespaces you will need to include are also listed in Listing 4-4.

Listing 4-4. Method to query the Azure SQL Database for the earthquake data

```
public List<Earthquake> GetEarthquakesFromSql(String queryString)
    {
        // Provide the following information
        string userName = <my Azure SQL Database username>;
        string password = <my Azure SQL Database password>;
        string dataSource = <my Azure SQL Server name>;
        string sampleDatabaseName = <my Azure SQL Database name>;
```

```csharp
// Create a connection string for the sample database
SqlConnectionStringBuilder connString2Builder;
connString2Builder = new SqlConnectionStringBuilder();
connString2Builder.DataSource = dataSource;
connString2Builder.InitialCatalog = sampleDatabaseName;
connString2Builder.Encrypt = true;
connString2Builder.TrustServerCertificate = false;
connString2Builder.UserID = userName;
connString2Builder.Password = password;

// Connect to the sample database and perform various operations
using (SqlConnection conn = new SqlConnection(connString2Builder.ToString()))
{
    SqlCommand cmd = conn.CreateCommand();
    conn.Open();
    cmd.CommandText = queryString;

    var data = new List<Earthquake>();
    using (SqlDataReader reader = cmd.ExecuteReader())
    {
        while (reader.Read())
        {

            var when = (DateTime)reader.GetValue(0);
            var position = SqlGeographyDeserialize(reader.GetSqlBytes(1));
            var where = new Location((double)position.Lat, (double)position.Long);
            var magnitude = (float)(double)reader.GetValue(2);
            var depth = (float)(double)reader.GetValue(3);
            var magType = (string)reader.GetValue(4);
            var nbStation = (int)reader.GetValue(5);
            var gap = (float)(double)reader.GetValue(6);
            var distance = (float)(double)reader.GetValue(7);
            var rms = (float)(double)reader.GetValue(8);
            var source = (string)reader.GetValue(9);
            var eventId = (string)reader.GetValue(10);
            var title = (string)reader.GetValue(11);

            data.Add(new Earthquake(when,
                                    where,
                                    depth,
                                    magnitude,
                                    magType,
                                    nbStation,
                                    gap,
                                    distance,
                                    rms,
                                    source,
                                    eventId,
                                    title));
        }
    }
```

```
                conn.Close();

                return data;
            }
        }
```

The implementation of GetEarthquakeDataBBox is essentially just as it was for GetEarthquakeData; however, the query string will differ in that we will add a filter to the query that defines the bounding box and filters the data to only return the entries that lie within the bounding box. The query string will have the following format:

DECLARE @g geography; SET @g=geography::STGeomFromText('POLYGON((<my bounding box coordinates>))', 4326); SELECT <desired fields> FROM <my SQL database table name> WHERE <my geo data field>.Filter(@g)=1"

Note how we're using the SQL extensions here–we create a polygon of our bounding coordinates and perform a geospatial query in our table.

In our case, we create the string as in Listing 4-5.

Listing 4-5. Request all the earthquake data from within a bounding box

```
public List<Earthquake> GetEarthquakeDataBBox(double TLLong, double TLLat, double BRLong,
double BRLat)
{
    string tableName = "earthquakeData";
    var selectString = "SELECT DateTime, " +
                       "Position, " +
                       "Magnitude, " +
                       "Depth, " +
                       "MagType, " +
                       "NbStation, " +
                       "Gap, " +
                       "Distance, " +
                       "RMS, " +
                       "Source, " +
                       "EventID, " +
                       "Title FROM " + tableName;

    string bboxString = "POLYGON((" +
                TLLong + " " + TLLat + ", " +
                BRLong + " " + TLLat + ", " +
                BRLong + " " + BRLat + ", " +
                TLLong + " " + BRLat + ", " +
                TLLong + " " + TLLat +
                "))";
    var setGeometry = "DECLARE @g geography; SET @g=geography::STGeomFromText
('" + bboxString + "', 4326); ";
    var queryFilter = " WHERE Position.Filter(@g)=1";

    var queryString = setGeometry + selectString + queryFilter;
    return GetEarthquakesFromSql(queryString);
}
```

7. You have now created your WCF service, and you can run it locally by selecting Debug ➤ Start. Visual Studio will launch the browser that will have your service running with a URL of `http://localhost:49717/Service1.svc` (the port number may be different). Now the service is running locally. See Figure 4-5.

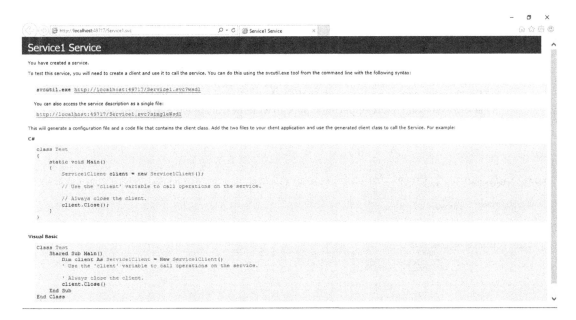

Figure 4-5. *WCF service created and running locally*

Although not necessary for implementation, we would like to draw your attention to the `ServiceDefinition.csdef` file. This file contains all the service definitions we talked about at the beginning of the chapter. You will note that the bindings and endpoints were all automatically generated when you created your solution. You can also specify the virtual machine size in this file. The default is set to small, but you may want to set it to extra small while testing, since the extra small VM has the lowest bill rate per usage.

Two other files were automatically generated: `ServiceConfiguration.Local.cscfg` and `ServiceConfiguration.Cloud.cscfg`. These files provide the configuration settings for your application, including the number of instances to run for each role. By default, the instance count is set to 1. We will leave that instance number at 1 for our sample codes, but for robustness, you may want to run multiple instances of the same role when you deploy your own applications.

If you were to open one of these files, it will resemble the following listing:

```
<?xml version="1.0" encoding="utf-8"?>

<ServiceConfiguration serviceName="WCFEarthquakeService" xmlns="http://schemas.
microsoft.com/ServiceHosting/2008/10/ServiceConfiguration" osFamily="4" osVersion="*"
schemaVersion="2015-04.2.6">
  <Role name="WCFServiceWebRole1">
    <Instances count="1" />
    <ConfigurationSettings>
```

```
    <Setting name="Microsoft.WindowsAzure.Plugins.Diagnostics.ConnectionString"
      value="UseDevelopmentStorage=true" />
    </ConfigurationSettings>
  </Role>
</ServiceConfiguration>
```

Hosting the WCF Service on Azure

1. You will need to publish the service package and service configuration package before you can deploy your service on Azure. Right-click on the WCFEarthquakeService project name in the Solution Explorer and select Package. A Package Microsoft Azure Application pop-up window will appear. See Figure 4-6.

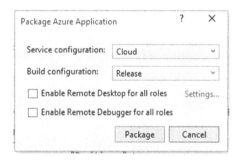

Figure 4-6. *Create Package Azure Application form*

As you will be deploying to Azure, you can leave the Service configuration as Cloud. Click Package. Visual Studio will open a folder that contains your two files: ServiceConfiguration.Cloud.cscfg and WCFEarthquakeService.cspkg, which are the configuration files and service package respectively. Take note of where these files are saved, as you will need them later.

2. Log in to your management portal for Microsoft Azure at azure.microsoft.com. You can click on Portal at the top of the page, or you can get there directly by going to http://manage.windowsazure.com.

3. Select New at the bottom of the page in order to create a new service.

4. Create a new custom cloud service. Note, you may find that some sites refer to this as a hosted service. See Figure 4-7.

Figure 4-7. *Create custom cloud service*

5. You will be asked to give a URL name to the service. We chose
    myEarthquakeService. Click Next. See Figure 4-8.

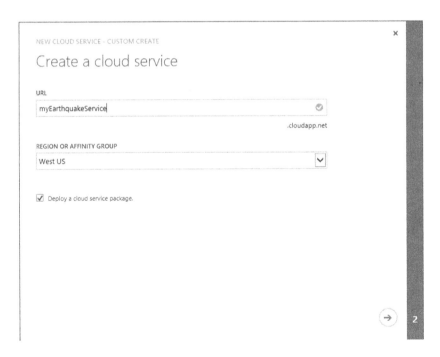

Figure 4-8. *Give the cloud service URL a name*

6. You can enter a deployment name for the service. It is here that you will upload the packages generated in Step 1. You can choose to deploy to the staging or production environment. We have chosen staging. Finally, recall that the default of the service you created was a single instance of the web role. If you did not change the number of instances to more than 1, then you will need to check "Deploy even if one or more roles contain a single instance" in order for your deployment to work. Click the check mark to create your cloud service. It may take a few minutes to finish the deployment. See Figure 4-9.

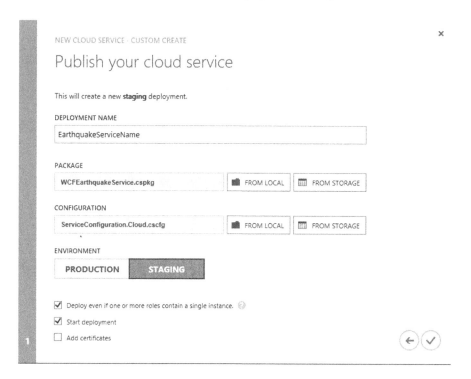

Figure 4-9. Create your cloud service

7. Once the service has been successfully created, you can click on the newly created service, myEarthquakeService, in the management portal to see more details. As we have chosen to deploy to the staging environment, click on Staging. If you scroll down the page, you will see a list of the details pertaining to this service. The status will be set to Running. It is also here that you will see the URL for the deployed service. It will be listed under Site URL, in the form: http://<guid>.cloudapp.net. If you click on the link, you will be brought to that page. From there you will be able to select your service, Service1.svc, so that you will now have your service open in the browser at: http://<guid>.cloudapp.net/Service1.svc. Take note of this URL as you will be calling it in your client application. Your WCF service is now running in Azure! If you deployed to Production rather than Staging then the URL will be http://<URLname>.cloudapp.net/Service1.svc.

Client Application

There are a variety of client applications that can call this WCF service. We will show you how to build one simple client application that runs locally on your machine.

1. Open Visual Studio and create a new project: File ➤ New ➤ Project. Under Template ➤ Visual C# ➤ Windows select Console Application. Name your application. We named ours getEarthquakeDataApp. Click OK.

2. In the Solution Explorer, right-click the project name and select Add Service Reference.

3. In the resulting pop-up window, in the Address textbox, enter the URL of your Azure-deployed WCF Service and click Go. (If you are running the service locally, then add that URL instead.) Your service will appear under Services. Click on Advanced. Recall that when you created your service, the service was returning a list of earthquakes. Change the Collection Type to System.Collections. Generic.List. Click OK. Click OK to add the Service Reference.

■ **Note**　You can always change the service reference configuration by right-clicking the service reference and selecting Configure Service Reference. If you make changes to the WCF service, do not forget to update your service by right-clicking on the service reference and selecting Update Service Reference.

---

4. Modify the Program.cs file to call your service. Our program is quite simple. It will first request all the earthquakes in the database from the WCF service, and then request all the earthquakes within a bounding box from the service; see the code in Listing 4-6. You will need to include the service reference and then create an instance of this service client. Once you've done so, you can use this service client object to call the methods in your WCF service. In our case they will be GetEarthquakeData and GetEarthquakeDataBBox. You will need to include the Earthquake class from Listing 4-2, without the data contracts. The class can also be found in Chapter 3 in the sample code.

Listing 4-6. Client application to call the WCF service

```
using System;
using System.Collections.Generic;
using getEarthquakeDataApp.ServiceReference1;

namespace getEarthquakeDataApp
{
    class Program
    {
        static void Main(string[] args)
        {
            Service1Client client = null;

            try
            {
                client = new Service1Client();
                var test = client.GetEarthquakeData();
```

```
                var data = new List<Earthquake>();
                foreach (var earthquake in test)
                {
                    var when = earthquake.When;
                    var where = earthquake.Location;
                    var magnitude = earthquake.Magnitude;
                    var depth = earthquake.Depth;
                    var magType = earthquake.MagType;
                    var nbStation = earthquake.NbStation;
                    var gap = earthquake.Gap;
                    var distance = earthquake.Distance;
                    var rms = earthquake.RMS;
                    var source = earthquake.Source;
                    var eventId = earthquake.EventID;
                    var title = earthquake.Title;
                    Console.WriteLine("{0}, {1}, {2}, {3}, {4}, {5}, {6}, {7}, {8}, {9},
{10}, {11}", when, where, magnitude, depth, magType, nbStation, gap, distance, rms, source,
eventId, title);
                    data.Add(new Earthquake(when, where, magnitude, depth, magType,
nbStation, gap, distance, rms, source, eventId, title));
                }

                var test2 = client.GetEarthquakeDataBBox(-145, 0, -75, 45);
                var data2 = new List<Earthquake>();
                foreach (var earthquake in test2)
                {
                    var when = earthquake.When;
                    var where = earthquake.Location;
                    var magnitude = earthquake.Magnitude;
                    var depth = earthquake.Depth;
                    var magType = earthquake.MagType;
                    var nbStation = earthquake.NbStation;
                    var gap = earthquake.Gap;
                    var distance = earthquake.Distance;
                    var rms = earthquake.RMS;
                    var source = earthquake.Source;
                    var eventId = earthquake.EventID;
                    var title = earthquake.Title;
                    Console.WriteLine("{0}, {1}, {2}, {3}, {4}, {5}, {6}, {7}, {8}, {9},
{10}, {11}", when, where, magnitude, depth, magType, nbStation, gap, distance, rms, source,
eventId, title);
                    data2.Add(new Earthquake(when, where, magnitude, depth, magType,
nbStation, gap, distance, rms, source, eventId, title));
                }
            }
            catch (Exception e)
            {
                Console.WriteLine("Exception encounter: {0}", e.Message);
            }
            finally
            {
```

```
            Console.WriteLine("Done!");
            Console.ReadLine();
            if (null != client)
            {
                client.Close();
            }
        }
    }
  }
}
```

A Note on Debugging

The majority of your debugging as you develop would be conveniently done if you run the service locally first. This will avoid having to deploy to Azure every time you make a slight change. It also ensures that you are not paying while you are developing and not actually needing the service to be up and running. Debugging a service that is deployed on Azure requires some setup.

1. To be able to see why your Azure service cannot run, you will need to add the following to your web.config file:

    ```
    <system.web>
      <customErrors mode="Off"/>
    </system.web>
    ```

    The element customErrors indicates whether filtered or complete exception information is returned by the server. There are three options for mode: Off, On, and RemoteOnly. The default is RemoteOnly, which returns complete exception information only to callers on the same machine. Setting customError to Off allows you to see the exceptions when your Azure-deployed service fails to run. When you click on the URL of the service, the browser will show you the exceptions rather than the running service.

2. If your service runs, when your client calls the service there may still be errors that you did not catch when debugging locally. You will want the client to be able to see these exceptions. In order to do so, you will need to turn the includeExceptionDetailInFaults on in your web.config file:

    ```
    <behavior name="metadataAndDebugEnabled">
      <serviceDebug
        includeExceptionDetailInFaults="true"
      />
      <serviceMetadata
        httpGetEnabled="true"
        httpGetUrl=""
      />
    </behavior>
    ```

Additionally, in `Service1.svc.cs`, you will add the following before you implement the service methods:

```
[ServiceBehavior(
    IncludeExceptionDetailInFaults = true
  )]
```

Setting `IncludeExceptionDetailInFaults` to `true` allows clients to obtain information on internal-service exceptions.

Wrapping Up

In this chapter, you learned how to create a WCF service that serves geospatial data from an Azure SQL database to clients. You then learned how to host that service on Azure and create a client application that calls the service. WCF may not be the only way to create service-oriented applications, but as you have seen in this chapter, it makes the development of such services straightforward and easy.

CHAPTER 5

■ ■ ■

Map Visualization with Bing Maps for the Web

We are now finally able to begin your first Bing Maps application with all the pieces you made in the previous chapters! In this chapter, you will learn how to visualize the earthquake data we collected in Chapter 3, using the WCF data service developed in Chapter 4 on the Azure-hosted, web-based Bing map created in Chapter 2.

We will begin by walking you through some basic Bing Maps API. In this book we are using the Bing Maps Ajax Control Version 7.0, which, in conjunction with the Bing Maps REST services, provides you with the ability to create web-based Bing Maps applications. The extensive API for these controls is available at the MSDN website: `http://bit.ly/1cCGT6R`. There is also an interactive SDK online that provides template code for much of the functionality: `http://bit.ly/1eAcEKz`.

Bing Maps Ajax Control Basics

In Chapter 2, you learned how to display a basic web-based Bing map and host it on Microsoft Azure. Recall that in order to display the map, you need your Bing Maps key, which you obtained in Chapter 2. You will then replace the string `'Your Bing Maps Key'` in the following command with your key:

```
map = new Microsoft.Maps.Map(document.getElementById('SDKmap'),
    {credentials: 'Your Bing Maps Key'});
```

The resulting map will look like that in Figure 5-1. This basic map serves as a jumping-off point for a variety of different map options and features. We will discuss a few of those options in the remainder of this chapter.

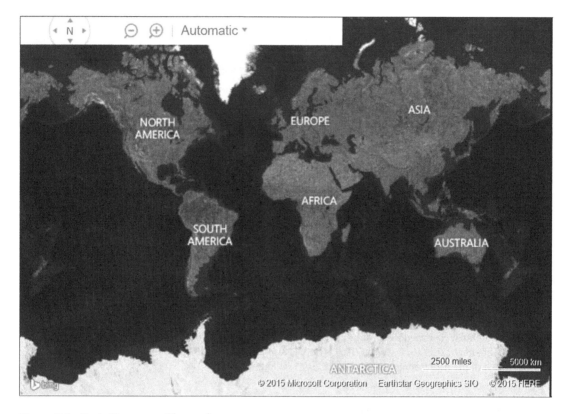

Figure 5-1. *Basic Bing map with map key*

Playing with the Map View

When the default map opens, it appears as in Figure 5-1. At times you may want the map to be centered at a different location. You can specify the map's center as follows:

```
map.setView({ center: new Microsoft.Maps.Location(47.6, -122.33) });
```

1. The map is now centered at a location somewhere near Seattle, Washington, USA, but will remain at the same zoom level as seen in Figure 5-2.

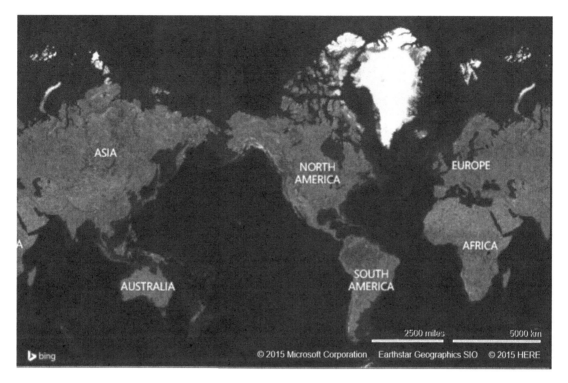

Figure 5-2. *Basic Bing map centered on Seattle, Washington, USA*

If we wanted to zoom in on the map, we could change the zoom by setting the zoom level in the setView command:

```
map.setView({ center: new Microsoft.Maps.Location(47.6, -122.33), zoom: 10});
```

The map will now be zoomed in at the Seattle location at the specified zoom level, as shown in Figure 5-3. Different zoom levels will reveal different levels of detail. For example, at this latitude and longitude, a zoom level of 16 will render the map with all the corresponding street names (not shown).

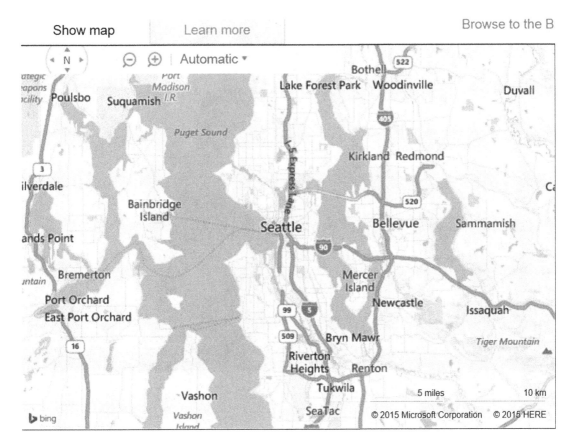

Figure 5-3. Basic map zoomed in on Seattle location at zoom level 10

Map Markers

The most common type of map marker is the basic pushpin. The basic pushpin can be added using the code in Listing 5-1. You will note that it is similar to the code for the basic map, with the addition of the following commands:

```
var pushpin = new Microsoft.Maps.Pushpin(map.getCenter(), null);
map.entities.push(pushpin);
```

A pushpin is created with the location set to the map center. The newly created pushpin is then pushed into the map, as seen in Figure 5-4.

Figure 5-4. Default pushpin with the location set to the center of the map

Listing 5-1. HTML code to insert a basic pushpin into the Bing map

```
<!DOCTYPE html PUBLIC "-//W3C//DTD XHTML 1.0 Transitional//EN" "http://www.w3.org/TR/xhtml1/
DTD/xhtml1-transitional.dtd">
<html>
    <head>
        <title>Add default pushpin</title>
        <meta http-equiv="Content-Type" content="text/html; charset=utf-8"/>
        <script type="text/javascript"
          src="http://ecn.dev.virtualearth.net/mapcontrol/mapcontrol.ashx?v=7.0">
                </script>
        <script type="text/javascript">
        var map = null;

        function getMap()
        {
          map = new Microsoft.Maps.Map(document.getElementById('myMap'),
            {credentials: 'Your Bing Maps Key'});
        }
```

```
    function addDefaultPushpin()
    {
      var pushpin= new Microsoft.Maps.Pushpin(map.getCenter(), null);
      map.entities.push(pushpin);
    }
    </script>
  </head>
  <body onload="getMap();">
    <div id='myMap' style="position:relative;
     width:400px; height:400px;"></div>
    <div>
        <input type="button" value="AddDefaultPushpin"
          onclick="addDefaultPushpin();" />
    </div>
  </body>
</html
```

Setting the Location of a Pushpin

If we wanted to specify the location of the pushpin to a location other than the center of the map, then we would change the create pushpin command to:

```
var pushpin = new Microsoft.Maps.Pushpin(
  new Microsoft.Maps.Location(myLatitude, myLongitude),
  null);
```

The arguments myLatitude and myLongitude are replaced with the corresponding latitude and longitude of the location at which you would like the pushpin to appear. You will notice that, thus far, the Microsoft.Maps.Pushpin command takes two arguments, the second of which we have left null. This is actually where we can put some additional pushpin options. A list of the options can be found here: http://bit.ly/1cnjUO3. For example, you can set the pushpin visibility to true or false, or even specify the pushpin height and width. An example of some pushpin options is as follows:

```
var pushpinOptions = { text: 'hi', visible: true };
var pushpin = new Microsoft.Maps.Pushpin(
  new Microsoft.Maps.Location(myLatitude, myLongitude),
  pushpinOptions);
```

The option being set is that the pushpin will place the string 'hi' within the pushpin, if the visibility is set to true. It will look as in Figure 5-5.

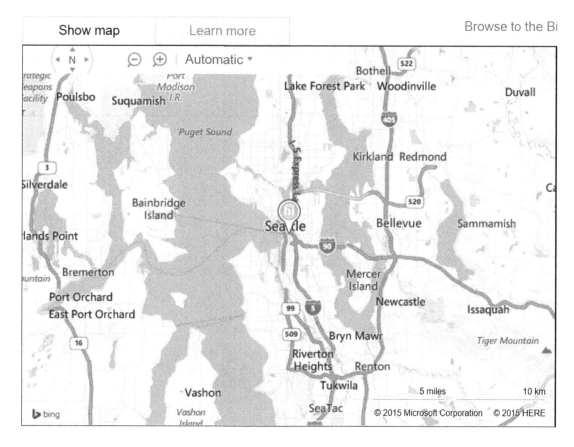

Figure 5-5. *Pushpin in Bing map with a location set and the text option turned on and set to 'hi'*

Polygons

Another possible option for Bing Maps is the ability to draw polygons on the map. The most basic polygon is a polyline. With the following code snippet we can draw a square around Union Square in San Francisco. We have also centered the map at Union Square and set the zoom level to 15 so that the polyline is visible. See the following:

```
map.entities.clear();
var polyline = new Microsoft.Maps.Polyline(
  [
    new Microsoft.Maps.Location(37.788327,-122.408447),
    new Microsoft.Maps.Location(37.788531,-122.406837),
    new Microsoft.Maps.Location(37.787607,-122.406676),
    new Microsoft.Maps.Location(37.787412,-122.408264),
    new Microsoft.Maps.Location(37.788327,-122.408447)
  ], null);
map.setView( { center: new Microsoft.Maps.Location(37.788327,-122.408447), zoom:15});
map.entities.push(polyline);
```

The polyline comprises four latitude and longitude pairs, with the first point being repeated at the end in order to close the loop: (37.788327,-122.408447), (37.788531,-122.406837), (37.787607,-122.406676), (37.787412,-122.408264). The resulting map appears as in Figure 5-6.

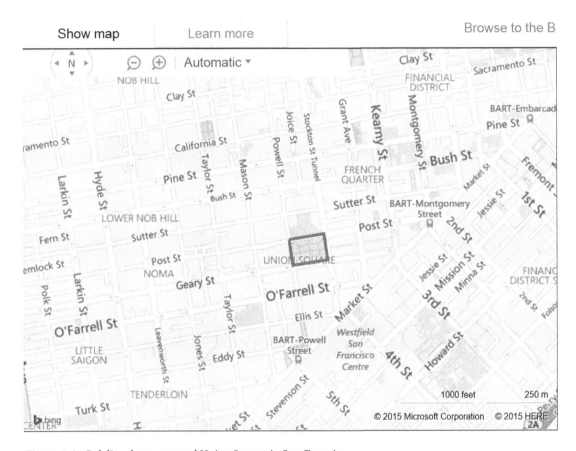

Figure 5-6. *Polyline drawn around Union Square in San Francisco*

If we wanted to draw a polygon instead, for example, we would use a polygon shape rather than a polyline. The code would change as follows:

```
map.entities.clear();
var polygon = new Microsoft.Maps.Polygon(
  [
    new Microsoft.Maps.Location(37.788327,-122.408447),
    new Microsoft.Maps.Location(37.788531,-122.406837),
    new Microsoft.Maps.Location(37.787607,-122.406676),
    new Microsoft.Maps.Location(37.787412,-122.408264),
    new Microsoft.Maps.Location(37.788327,-122.408447)
  ], null);
map.setView( { center: new Microsoft.Maps.Location(37.788327,-122.408447), zoom:15});
map.entities.push(polygon);
```

And the resulting polygon on the map will appear as in Figure 5-7. You'll note that because we have used the same location pairs, the shape remains the same as in Figure 5-6; however, it is now shaded in. There are other options that you can apply to the polygons, such as adjusting the colors, the opacity of the fill color, and the line thickness, and we encourage you to see the API for more information on these options.

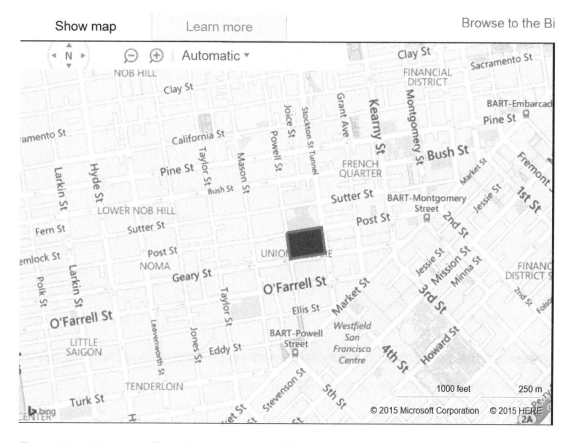

Figure 5-7. A Bing map with a polygon drawn around Union Square in San Francisco

Putting It All Together

Now that we have learned some basic map options, we are ready to build our sample code for this chapter. In this sample application, we will be displaying the earthquake data that we retrieved in Chapter 3 on a web-based Bing map using pushpins.

Begin by setting up your solution:

1. Create an empty project in C# in Visual Studio (File ➤ New Project). Under C# ➤ Web, select ASP.NET Web Application. See Figure 5-8.

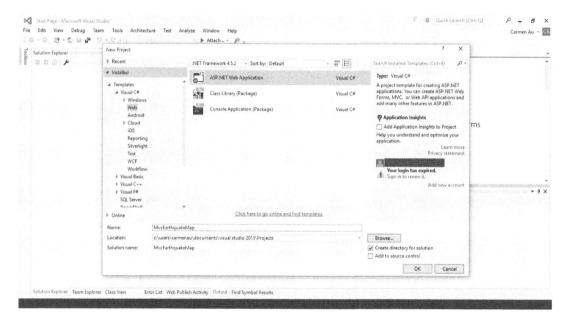

Figure 5-8. *Create an ASP.NET Web Application in Visual Studio 2015*

2. Name this application MvcEarthquakeMap and click OK.

3. Select an empty project template and be sure to check MVC under "Add folders and core references for." Click OK, and Visual Studio will have created all the dummy folders and files for your project. See Figure 5-9.

Figure 5-9. *Select an empty MVC template*

You have now created a Model-View-Controller project. We will not be covering the specifics of MVC paradigms in this book; however, we will provide a simple explanation that pertains to our particular example. In Figure 5-10, we have drawn how our MVC is used.

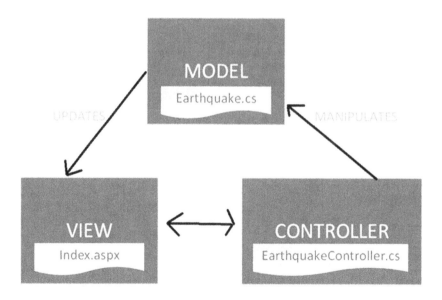

Figure 5-10. *The Model-View-Controller used in this sample application*

Create the Model

We begin with an Earthquake model. This model is a basic class that contains the data types that are required to represent an earthquake's data. We used this class in Chapter 3, and relist the code here for clarity in Listing 5-2. Right-click on the folder Models in the Solution Explorer of Visual Studio and select Add ➤ Class. Name this class Earthquake.cs and paste Listing 5-2 over the created class.

Listing 5-2. Earthquake.cs

```
using System;
using Microsoft.Maps.MapControl.WPF;

namespace MvcEarthquakeMap.Models
{
    public class Earthquake
    {
        public DateTime When { get; set; }
        public Location Location { get; set; }
        public float Depth { get; set; }
        public float Magnitude { get; set; }
        public string MagType { get; set; }
        public int NbStation { get; set; }
        public float Gap { get; set; }
        public float Distance { get; set; }
        public float RMS { get; set; }
        public string Source { get; set; }
        public string EventID { get; set; }
        public string Title { get; set; }
        public string Description { get; set; }

        public Earthquake(DateTime when, Location where,
            float depth, float magnitude, string magType,
            int nbStation, float gap, float distance,
            float rms, string source, string eventId,
            string title, string description = "")
        {
            When = when;
            Location = where;
            Depth = depth;
            Magnitude = magnitude;
            MagType = magType;
            NbStation = nbStation;
            Gap = gap;
            Distance = distance;
            RMS = rms;
            Source = source;
            EventID = eventId;
            Title = title;
            Description = description;
        }
    }
}
```

You will need to add the `Microsoft.Maps.MapControl.WPF` reference by right-clicking References and selecting Add Reference.

Loading the Earthquake Data (The Controller)

Once the `Earthquake` model is created, you need to load the earthquake data into it. This step is done in the controller, which you create by right-clicking Controllers and selecting Add ➤ Controller. Select the empty controller and name it `EarthquakeController.cs` (see Figure 5-11).

Figure 5-11. *Select the empty MVC 5 controller*

Once you select OK, the corresponding stub code will be created. You now need to add the namespace for the `Earthquake` model at the top of the page:

```
using MvcEarthquakeMap.Models;
```

In Chapter 4, we discussed how to create a WCF data service that pulled the earthquake data from the SQL database. We will assume that this data loaded magically into a `List` called `quakes` in the function `GetLocations()`:

```
public ActionResult Index()
{
        List<Earthquake> quakes = GetLocations();
        return View(quakes);
}
```

We then pass the data structure containing the `Earthquake` model to the view.

Displaying the Earthquake Data (The View)

To create the view, you can right-click on the Controller function:

```
Public ActionResult Index()
```

And select Add View. Leave the name as Index, set the template to Empty, check "Create as a partial view," and set Earthquake (MvcEarthquakeMap.Models) as the model class, as in Figure 5-12.

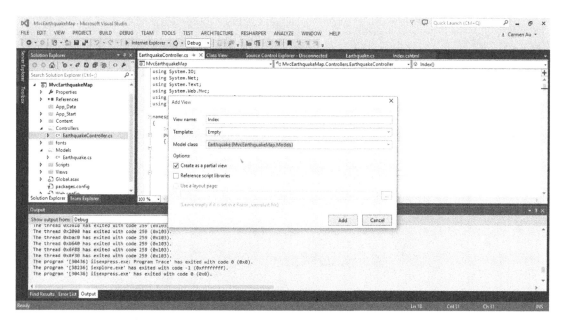

Figure 5-12. *Creating the view from the controller*

Once you click Add, the stub code for the view will be created. At the top of Index.cshtml, you will find the following line of code:

```
@model MvcEarthquakeMap.Models.Earthquake
```

By including this, you have enabled the model to be visible in this view. You will remember, however, that we passed a list of the Earthquake models to the view, and not simply the Earthquake model alone. Thus, in Listing 5-3 we change that code to reflect the IEnumerable data structure:

Listing 5-3. Listing for the view that displays the Earthquake data in the map

```
@model IEnumerable<MvcEarthquakeMap.Models.Earthquake>

@{
    Layout = null;
}
<!DOCTYPE HTML PUBLIC "-//W3C//DTD XHTML 1.0 Transitional//EN" "http://www.w3.org/TR/xhtml1/
DTD/xhtml1-transitional.dtd">
```

```html
<html>
<head>
    <title>Add default pushpin</title>
    <meta http-equiv="Content-Type" content="text/html; charset=utf-8" />
    <script type="text/javascript" src="http://ecn.dev.virtualearth.net/mapcontrol/
    mapcontrol.ashx?v=7.0"></script>
    <script type="text/javascript">
        var map = null;

        function getMap() {
            map = new Microsoft.Maps.Map(document.getElementById('myMap'), { credentials:
            <my bing map credentials> });
        }

        function addEarthquakePushpins() {
            @foreach (var item in Model) {
                @:addPushpin(@item.Location.Latitude, @item.Location.Longitude,
                         '@item.Magnitude');
                    }
        }

        function addPushpin(lat, lon, magnitude) {
            var pushpinOptions = { text: magnitude, visible: true};
            var pushpin = new Microsoft.Maps.Pushpin(
              new Microsoft.Maps.Location(lat, lon), pushpinOptions);
            map.entities.push(pushpin);
        }

    </script>
</head>
<body onload="getMap();">
    <div id='myMap' style="position:relative;
     width:1250px; height:600px;"></div>
    <div>
        <input type="button" value="AddEarthquakePushpins"
         onclick="addEarthquakePushpins();" />
    </div>
</body>
</html>
```

The majority of this code listing will be familiar from Chapter 2, as the basic map remains the same. The main difference is the addition of the functions addEarthquakePushpins() and addPushpin(), and the button AddEarthquakePushpins that calls it. In the function addEarthquakePushpins(), we iterate through the list of Earthquake models and, for each item, we call addPushpin(), passing the location and magnitude of each item to it. In addPushpin(), a pushpin is added at the location of the Earthquake item. You will note the use of the @ symbol. This symbol is used for the model, and is required for referencing the model in your script.

Additionally, we added a pushpin option that added the corresponding magnitude of each earthquake object as the text of the pushpin.

If you run this project, you will see a Bing map like that in Figure 5-13 that displays the earthquake data that we retrieved in Chapters 3 and 4. (Note: your pushpins will be in different locations than ours, as your earthquake data will not be the same as ours.)

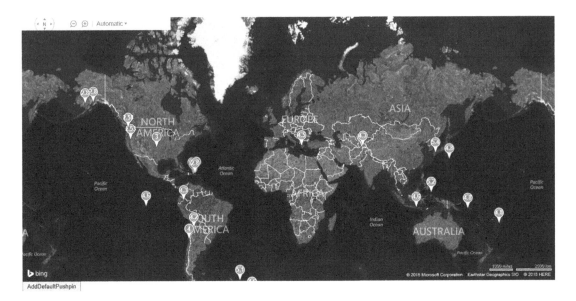

Figure 5-13. *Bing map displaying earthquake data at their locations with their corresponding magnitudes*

Wrapping Up

Bing Maps Ajax Control allows you to create web-based Bing Maps applications with minimal effort. The online Interactive SDK creates the majority of the code snippets you will need, so much of the work required can be done by copy and paste! If you have a basic understanding of ASP.NET and MVC programming, a simple application such as the sample application in this chapter can be written in a couple of hours. In this chapter, we covered pushpins and polygons. In the subsequent chapter, we will be showing you how you can go even further with the APIs and build rich map applications using Bing Maps!

CHAPTER 6

■ ■ ■

Doing More with Bing Maps

So you have now learned to build your first Bing Maps web application. You can display geodata on a Bing map using pushpins. You even learned how to draw some basic geometric shapes. Now it's time for the fun stuff! Bing Maps can go so much further than the basic application we showed you in Chapter 5. Using Bing Maps REST (Representational State Transfer) Services, you'll be able to calculate routes between waypoints, or query for traffic incidents and much more. The Bing Maps REST Services API consists of the following APIs:

- **Location API**: Finds a location based on an address or query

- **Elevations API**: Returns the elevation of a location, path, or given Earth area

- **Imagery API**: Returns a static map or Bing Maps imagery information

- **Route API**: Calculates routes between two waypoints, or from a major road. You can also select either driving or walking directions.

- **Traffic API**: Used to get traffic information or other road incidents, such as construction.

In addition to REST services, Bing Maps AJAX Control v7 offers modules that provide much of the same functionality without needing to go through REST services. For example, rather than querying the REST service for routes, you can also load the `Bing.Maps.Directions` module and request routes using that instead. Some available modules are directions module, overlays module, and theme modules; however, you can also download custom modules or create your own.

In this chapter, we will walk you through a few key services and other modules you can add for additional features and functionality. The functionalities we cover in this book are:

- **Location**: Determine a location based on an address or point of interest

- **Routing**: Determine the route between the given waypoints

- **Traffic**: Determine the current traffic conditions

- **Theming**: Applying the latest Bing Maps site designs in your own application

In addition, we will go into more detail as to the semantics of the Bing Maps REST APIs in Chapter 9, and will discuss the Elevations and Imagery APIs in more detail there.

We will also show you how to create and add a custom module. There are, of course, other things you can do with Bing Maps; however, the APIs for those are similar enough to the ones we will cover in this chapter that we refer you to the Bing Maps APIs online for the specifics.

Location

The first location-type question you might ask is "Where is it?" For example, if we were to have the string "Beijing, China", we would like to be able to determine a latitude and longitude based on this query string. To answer this question, we use the Bing Maps REST Services and query for the location. Of course, another location-type question we might ask is "Where am I?" That question can be answered by the GeoLocationProvider class that is provided by the AJAX Control. We will walk you through answering these two questions in the following sections.

Where Is It?

The Location API gives you the ability to return the location in terms of latitude and longitude based on a query string. The REST call for such a query will appear as follows:

```
var searchRequest = 'http://dev.virtualearth.net/REST/v1/Locations/' + queryLocation +
'?output=json&jsonp=searchServiceCallback&key=' + 'Your Bing Map Key';
```

The query location string, queryLocation, can be something like "Seattle, WA". The Bing Map REST service will return either an XML or JSON response object. In this case, we have specified that a JSON object be returned, as we are working with Javascript code. Moreover, in the query, we have specified the function callback to be searchServiceCallback.

Once you have the entire query search string, you pass this string, searchRequest, to the script, which appears as follows:

```
var mapscript = document.createElement('script');
mapscript.type = 'text/javascript';
mapscript.src = searchRequest;
document.getElementById('myMap').appendChild(mapscript)
```

You create a script document element and set the type as Javascript, then you simply specify the source to be your query string. Let us walk you through a sample application that queries the Location REST API for locations and displays the results with pushpins on a map.

Sample Location Query Application

Once again, we follow the standard MVC model from Chapter 5. Create a model named GeoLocation and paste code Listing 6-1 into it.

Listing 6-1. GeoLocation.cs. Model for a geo location

```
using System;
using System.Collections.Generic;
using System.Linq;
using System.Web;
using Microsoft.Maps.MapControl.WPF;

namespace MvcBingMapLocationByQuery.Models
{
    public class GeoLocation
    {
```

```
        public string LocationName { get; set; }
        public string City { get; set; }
        public Location Location { get; set; }

        public GeoLocation(string locationName, string city, Location where)
        {
            LocationName = locationName;
            City = city;
            Location = where;
        }
    }
}
```

Note, you should be adding the reference for `Microsoft.Maps.MapControl.WPF`. The model will be populated by the controller, which you create and name `HomeController.cs`; then you paste Listing 6-2 into it.

Listing 6-2. HomeController.cs controller populates the model class with geo-location data and passes the data to the view

```
using System;
using System.Collections.Generic;
using System.Linq;
using System.Web;
using System.Web.Mvc;
using MvcBingMapLocationByQuery.Models;
using Microsoft.Maps.MapControl.WPF;

namespace MvcBingMapLocationByQuery.Controllers
{
    public class HomeController : Controller
    {
        //
        // GET: /Home/

        public ActionResult Index()
        {
            var locations = GetLocations();
            return View(locations);
        }

        public List<GeoLocation> GetLocations()
        {
            var locations = new List<GeoLocation>();
            var loc1 = new Location(37.788302, -122.408513);
            var geoLoc1 = new GeoLocation("Union Square", "San Francisco", loc1);
            var loc2 = new Location(37.436703, -122.160273);
            var geoLoc2 = new GeoLocation("Stanford University", "Palo Alto", loc2);
            locations.Add(geoLoc1);
            locations.Add(geoLoc2);
```

```
        return locations;
    }


  }
}
```

Finally, you right-click on the `Index()` function declaration and add a view, `Index.cshtml`. As in Chapter 5, you will want to create a strongly typed view to the `GeoLocation` model. Once this is created, you can paste Listing 6-3.

Listing 6-3. Index.cshtml displays the map with the pushpins indicating the locations that result from the query strings

```
@using System.Web.Razor
@model IEnumerable<MvcBingMapLocationByQuery.Models.GeoLocation>

@{
    ViewBag.Title = "Index";
}

<!DOCTYPE HTML PUBLIC "-//W3C//DTD XHTML 1.0 Transitional//EN" "http://www.w3.org/TR/xhtml1/
DTD/xhtml1-transitional.dtd">
<html>
<head>
    <title>Find a location by query</title>
    <meta http-equiv="Content-Type" content="text/html; charset=utf-8" />
    <script type="text/javascript" src="http://ecn.dev.virtualearth.net/mapcontrol/
    mapcontrol.ashx?v=7.0"></script>
    <script type="text/javascript">
    var map = null;
    var query;
    var latitude;
    var longitude;
    function getMap() {
        map = new Microsoft.Maps.Map(document.getElementById('myMap'), { credentials: 'Your
        Bing Map Key' });
    }

    function findLocation() {

        @foreach (var item in Model)
            {
                @:mapLocation('@item.City', @item.Location.Latitude,
                @item.Location.Longitude);
            }
    }

        function mapLocation(city, lat, lon) {
            query = city;
            latitude = lat;
            longitude = lon;
            map.getCredentials(callSearchService);
        }
```

```
    function callSearchService(credentials) {
        var searchRequest = 'https://dev.virtualearth.net/REST/v1/Locations/' + query + '?
        output=json&jsonp=searchServiceCallback&key=' + credentials;
        var mapscript = document.createElement('script');
        mapscript.type = 'text/javascript';
        mapscript.src = searchRequest;
        document.getElementById('myMap').appendChild(mapscript)
    }

    function searchServiceCallback(result) {
        var output = document.getElementById("output");
        if (output) {
            while (output.hasChildNodes()) {
                output.removeChild(output.lastChild);
            }
        }
        var resultsHeader = document.createElement("h5");
        output.appendChild(resultsHeader);

        if (result &&
            result.resourceSets &&
            result.resourceSets.length > 0 &&
            result.resourceSets[0].resources &&
            result.resourceSets[0].resources.length > 0) {
            resultsHeader.innerHTML = "Bing Maps REST Search API  <br/>  Found location " +
            result.resourceSets[0].resources[0].name;
            map.setView({ center: new Microsoft.Maps.Location(latitude,longitude), zoom: 9 });
            var location = new Microsoft.Maps.Location(result.resourceSets[0].resources[0].
            point.coordinates[0], result.resourceSets[0].resources[0].point.coordinates[1]);
            var pushpin = new Microsoft.Maps.Pushpin(location);
            map.entities.push(pushpin);
        }
        else {
            if (typeof (response) == 'undefined' || response == null) {
                alert("Invalid credentials or no response");
            }
            else {
                if (typeof (response) != 'undefined' && response && result && result.
                errorDetails) {
                    resultsHeader.innerHTML = "Message :" + response.errorDetails[0];
                }
                alert("No results for the query");

            }
        }
    }

    </script>
</head>
```

```
<body onload="getMap();">
    <div id='myMap' style="position:relative; width:1000px; height:500px;"></div>
    <div>
        <input type="button" value="FindLocation" onclick="findLocation();" />
    </div>
    <div id="output"></div>
</body>
</html>
```

In the function findLocations, we get the query names of 'San Francisco' and 'Palo Alto' and then pass these names to the function callSearchService, which performs the REST query. Finally, the function searchServiceCallback the map view and adds a pushpin at the resulting locations. Figure 6-1 shows the final output of this sample application.

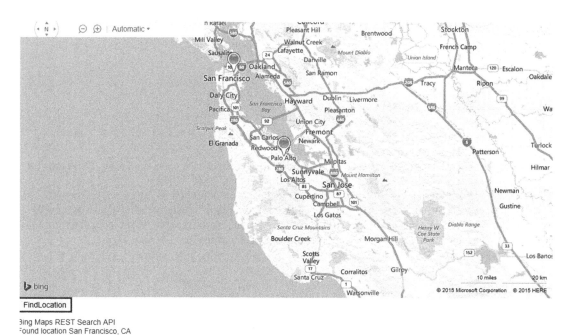

Figure 6-1. *Location results for query of San Francisco and Palo Alto*

■ **Note**   Using the model (GeoLocation.cs) in the view (Index.cshtml) requires the use of the character '@'. You will often partition off an area for which you will be using the model. In Listing 6-1, the model is used within the @foreach statement. Unfortunately, the Microsoft.Maps reference is not understood within that statement, or any section that uses the model. In order to get around this, we pull the values from the model and pass them to a separate function that can use the Microsoft.Maps reference.

Where Am I?

The GeoLocationProvider class will return the user's current location with compatible browsers, which support the W3C GeoLocation API (http://dev.w3.org/geo/api/spec-source.html). In Listing 6-4, we provide the code for requesting the user's location. The main difference between this code listing and previous view listings are the following commands:

```
var geoLocationProvider = new Microsoft.Maps.GeoLocationProvider(map);
geoLocationProvider.getCurrentPosition();
```

We instantiate the GeoLocationProvider class and initialize it with our map. Then we call getCurrentPosition to return the position. In Figure 6-2, we show you the resulting map, assuming the user was located on Stanford campus.

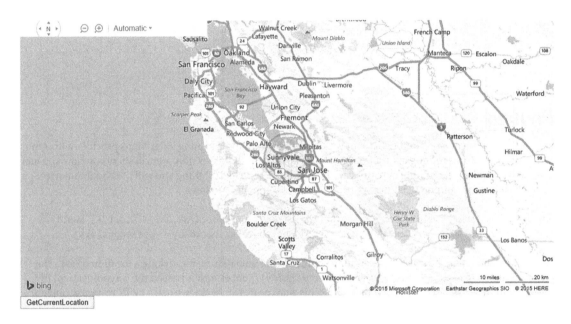

Figure 6-2. *User's geo location displayed on a Bing map*

Listing 6-4. Return the user's current location and display it on a map

```
<!DOCTYPE HTML PUBLIC "-//W3C//DTD XHTML 1.0 Transitional//EN" "http://www.w3.org/TR/xhtml1/
DTD/xhtml1-transitional.dtd">
<html>
<head>
    <title>Get location</title>
    <meta http-equiv="Content-Type" content="text/html; charset=utf-8" />
    <script type="text/javascript" src="http://ecn.dev.virtualearth.net/mapcontrol/
    mapcontrol.ashx?v=7.0"></script>
    <script type="text/javascript">
        var map = null;
```

```
        function getMap() {
            map = new Microsoft.Maps.Map(document.getElementById('myMap'), { credentials:
            'Your Bing Map Key' });
        }

        function getCurrentLocation() {
            var geoLocationProvider = new Microsoft.Maps.GeoLocationProvider(map);
            geoLocationProvider.getCurrentPosition();
        }
    </script>
</head>
<body onload="getMap();">
    <div id='myMap' style="position:relative; width:1000px; height:500px;"></div>
    <div>
        <input type="button" value="GetCurrentLocation" onclick="getCurrentLocation();" />
    </div>
    <div id='output'> </div>
</body>
</html>
```

Routing

Perhaps one of the most common tasks for which people use maps is routing. Bing Maps provides a Routing REST API that returns routing instructions between waypoints. In this section, we will show you how you can use this API to integrate routing in your own map applications. The first thing you will need to familiarize yourself with is the Routing REST query string, which will appear as follows:

```
var routeRequest = 'http://dev.virtualearth.net/REST/v1/Routes?wp.0=' + start + '&wp.1=' +
end + '&routePathOutput=Points&output=json&jsonp=routeCallback&key=' + credentials;
```

You will note that the query string is quite similar to the query string for making a location query. The request is made to http://dev.virtualearth.net/REST/v1/Routes and is passed the waypoints (wp) in question. In this case, we have added two waypoints, start and end. Again, we use a JSON response object. The query string is then passed to the Javascript in the same fashion as with the location query:

```
var mapscript = document.createElement('script');
mapscript.type = 'text/javascript';
mapscript.src = routeRequest;
document.getElementById('myMap').appendChild(mapscript);
```

Sample Routing Query Application

The sample will use much of the same code as the Location Query sample application did. The model will be the same GeoLocation.cs model from Listing 6-1, and the controller will be the same as Listing 6-2. The main difference will be in the view, which will now include the code from Listing 6-5:

Listing 6-5. Index.cshtml. View to display map with routing instructions

```
@model IEnumerable<MvcBingMapRouting.Models.GeoLocation>

<!DOCTYPE html>

<html>
<head>
    <title>Find directions</title>
    <meta http-equiv="Content-Type" content="text/html; charset=utf-8" />
    <script type="text/javascript" src="http://ecn.dev.virtualearth.net/mapcontrol/
    mapcontrol.ashx?v=7.0"></script>
    <script type="text/javascript">
        var map = null;
        var end;
        var start;

        function getMap() {
            map = new Microsoft.Maps.Map(document.getElementById('myMap'), { credentials:
            'Your Bing Map Key' });
        }


        function callRouteService(credentials) {
            var routeRequest = 'http://dev.virtualearth.net/REST/v1/Routes?wp.0=' + start
            + '&wp.1=' + end + '&routePathOutput=Points&output=json&jsonp=routeCallback&k
            ey=' + credentials;
            var mapscript = document.createElement('script');
            mapscript.type = 'text/javascript';
            mapscript.src = routeRequest;
            document.getElementById('myMap').appendChild(mapscript);
        }

        function routeCallback(result) {
            var output = document.getElementById("output");
            if (output) {
                while (output.hasChildNodes()) {
                    output.removeChild(output.lastChild);
                }
                var resultsHeader = document.createElement("h5");
                var resultsList = document.createElement("ol");
                output.appendChild(resultsHeader);
                output.appendChild(resultsList);
            }
```

```
if (result && result.resourceSets && result.resourceSets.length > 0 && result.
resourceSets[0].resources && result.resourceSets[0].resources.length > 0) {
    resultsHeader.innerHTML = "Bing Maps REST Route API  <br/>  Route from " +
    result.resourceSets[0].resources[0].routeLegs[0].startLocation.name + " to "
    + result.resourceSets[0].resources[0].routeLegs[0].endLocation.name;
    var resultsListItem = null;

    for (var i = 0; i < result.resourceSets[0].resources[0].routeLegs[0].
    itineraryItems.length; ++i) {
        resultsListItem = document.createElement("li");
        resultsList.appendChild(resultsListItem);
        resultStr = result.resourceSets[0].resources[0].routeLegs[0].
        itineraryItems[i].instruction.text;
        resultsListItem.innerHTML = resultStr;
    }
    var bbox = result.resourceSets[0].resources[0].bbox;
    var viewBoundaries = Microsoft.Maps.LocationRect.fromLocations(new
    Microsoft.Maps.Location(bbox[0], bbox[1]), new Microsoft.Maps.
    Location(bbox[2], bbox[3]));
    map.setView({ bounds: viewBoundaries });
    var routeline = result.resourceSets[0].resources[0].routePath.line; var
    routepoints = new Array();
    for (var i = 0; i < routeline.coordinates.length; i++) {
        routepoints[i] = new Microsoft.Maps.Location(routeline.coordinates[i]
        [0], routeline.coordinates[i][1]);
    }
    var routeshape = new Microsoft.Maps.Polyline(routepoints, { strokeColor: new
    Microsoft.Maps.Color(200, 0, 0, 200) });

    var startPushpinOptions = { anchor: new Microsoft.Maps.Point(10, 32) };
    var startPin = new Microsoft.Maps.Pushpin(new Microsoft.Maps.
    Location(routeline.coordinates[0][0], routeline.coordinates[0][1]),
    startPushpinOptions);

    var endPushpinOptions = { anchor: new Microsoft.Maps.Point(10, 32) };
    var endPin = new Microsoft.Maps.Pushpin(new Microsoft.Maps.
    Location(routeline.coordinates[routeline.coordinates.length - 1]
    [0], routeline.coordinates[routeline.coordinates.length - 1][1]),
    endPushpinOptions);
    map.entities.push(startPin);
    map.entities.push(endPin);
    map.entities.push(routeshape);
}

else {
    if (typeof (result.errorDetails) != 'undefined') {
        resultsHeader.innerHTML = result.errorDetails[0];
    }
    alert("No Route found");
}
}
```

```
        function route(startPoint, endPoint) {
            start = startPoint;
            end = endPoint;
            map.getCredentials(callRouteService);
        }
        function getDirections() {
            @{
                var startName = Model.ElementAt(0).LocationName;
                var startCity = Model.ElementAt(0).City;
                var endName = Model.ElementAt(1).LocationName;
                var endCity = Model.ElementAt(1).City;
                @:route('@startName, ' + '@startCity', '@endName, ' + '@endCity');
            }
        }

    </script>
</head>
<body onload="getMap();">
    <div id='myMap' style="position: relative; width: 1000px; height: 500px;"></div>
    <div>
        <input type="button" value="GetDirections" onclick="getDirections();" />
    </div>
    <div id="output"></div>

</body>
</html>
```

In this sample application, we pass the view two waypoints, Union Square in San Francisco and Stanford University in Palo Alto, along with their corresponding locations. The view parses these locations and requests routing instructions between the waypoints. With routeCallback(), the map is populated with pushpins from one waypoint to the other, and a polyline shape is drawn to reflect the routing directions by connecting the points along the routeline. You will recall that we covered how to draw polylines in Chapter 5, and now you know why! The result of this sample application will look like Figure 6-3.

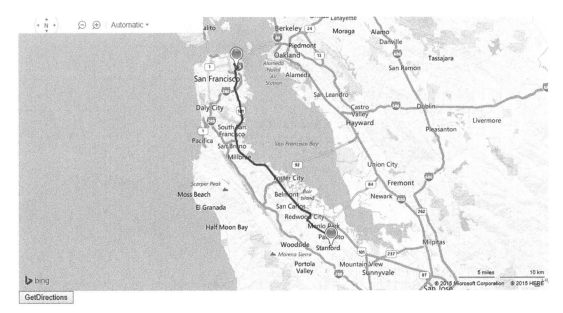

Bing Maps REST Route API
Route from Union Square, CA to Stanford University, CA

1. Depart Geary St toward Powell St
2. Turn left onto Mason St
3. Turn left onto O'Farrell St
4. Turn right onto Stockton St, and then immediately turn left onto 4th St
5. Take ramp right and follow signs for I-80 West
6. Keep straight onto US-101 S
7. At exit 408, take ramp right for CA-84 West toward Woodside Road
8. Bear right onto CA-84 W / Woodside Rd
9. Take ramp right toward El Camino Real South
10. Turn right onto Redwood Ave, and then immediately turn right onto CA-82 S / El Camino Real
11. Turn right onto Galvez St
12. Arrive at Stanford University, CA

Figure 6-3. *Routing directions between Union Square, San Francisco, and Stanford University, Palo Alto*

Alternatively, rather than using the REST Services, you can load the `Directions` module.

Directions Module

Using the `Directions` module, you can get routing information. In Listing 6-6, we show you how to get driving directions using the module. In order to use this module, you must first load the module. In the function `createDirections`, you will find the command to load the directions module:

```
Microsoft.Maps.loadModule('Microsoft.Maps.Directions', { callback: createDrivingRoute })
```

This command then calls the function that will create waypoints and set them to be the start and end points of the route. You may, of course, have additional waypoints along the way. This example uses the same start and end points as in the previous example. You will note that you can set a waypoint to either an address or to a specific latitude and longitude.

Listing 6-6. Creating driving directions using the Directions module

```
@model IEnumerable<MvcBingMapsDirections.Models.GeoLocation>

@{
    ViewBag.Title = "Index";
}

<!DOCTYPE HTML PUBLIC "-//W3C//DTD XHTML 1.0 Transitional//EN" "http://www.w3.org/TR/xhtml1/
DTD/xhtml1-transitional.dtd">
<html>
<head>
    <title>Create Driving Route</title>
    <meta http-equiv="Content-Type" content="text/html; charset=utf-8" />
    <script type="text/javascript" src="http://ecn.dev.virtualearth.net/mapcontrol/
    mapcontrol.ashx?v=7.0"></script>
    <script type="text/javascript">
        var map = null;
        var directionsManager;
        var directionsErrorEventObj;
        var directionsUpdatedEventObj;
        var start;
        var end;

        function getMap() {
            map = new Microsoft.Maps.Map(document.getElementById('myMap'), { credentials:
            'Your Bing Map Key' });
        }

        function createDirectionsManager() {

            if (!directionsManager) {
                directionsManager = new Microsoft.Maps.Directions.DirectionsManager(map);
            }

            directionsManager.resetDirections();
            directionsErrorEventObj = Microsoft.Maps.Events.addHandler(directionsManager,
            'directionsError');
            directionsUpdatedEventObj = Microsoft.Maps.Events.addHandler(directionsManager,
            'directionsUpdated');
        }

        function createDrivingRoute() {
            if (!directionsManager) { createDirectionsManager(); }
            directionsManager.resetDirections();
            // Set Route Mode to driving
            directionsManager.setRequestOptions({ routeMode: Microsoft.Maps.Directions.
            RouteMode.driving });
            var waypoint1 = new Microsoft.Maps.Directions.Waypoint({ address: start });
            directionsManager.addWaypoint(waypoint1);
            var waypoint2 = new Microsoft.Maps.Directions.Waypoint({ address: end });
```

```
                directionsManager.addWaypoint(waypoint2);
                // Set the element in which the itinerary will be rendered
                directionsManager.setRenderOptions({ itineraryContainer: document.getElementById
                ('directionsItinerary') });
                directionsManager.calculateDirections();
            }

        function createDirections() {
            @{
                var startName = Model.ElementAt(0).LocationName;
                var startCity = Model.ElementAt(0).City;
                var endName = Model.ElementAt(1).LocationName;
                var endCity = Model.ElementAt(1).City;
                @:direction('@startName, ' + '@startCity', '@endName, ' + '@endCity');
              }
        }

        function direction(startPoint, endPoint) {
            start = startPoint;
            end = endPoint;
            if (!directionsManager) {
                Microsoft.Maps.loadModule('Microsoft.Maps.Directions', { callback:
                createDrivingRoute });
            }
            else {
                createDrivingRoute();
            }
        }
    </script>
</head>
<body onload="getMap();">
    <div id='myMap' style="position:relative; width:1000px; height:500px;"></div>
    <div>
        <input type="button" value="CreateDrivingRoute" onclick="createDirections();" />
    </div>
    <div id='directionsItinerary'> </div>
</body>
</html>
```

In Figure 6-4, we show you the resulting map and directions.

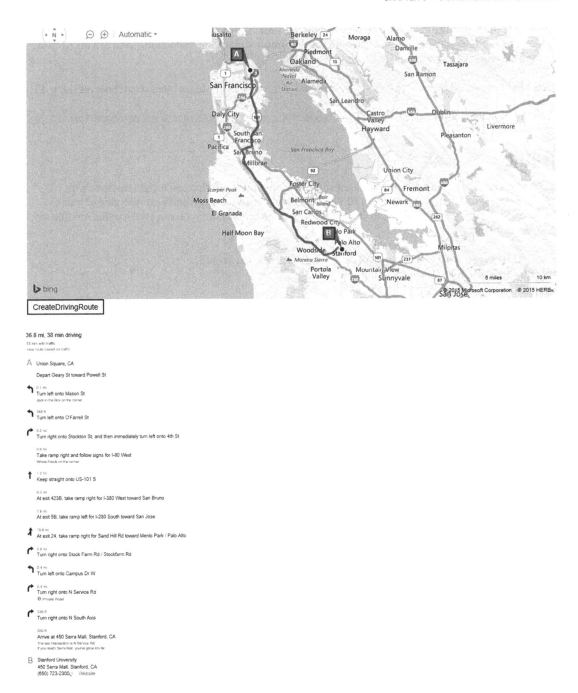

Figure 6-4. *Driving directions using the Directions module*

Rather than driving directions, you may want to get walking or transit directions instead. With the
Directions module, you are able to do so quite easily. Simply change the route mode from driving to either
walking or transit, as follows:

```
directionsManager.setRequestOptions({ routeMode: Microsoft.Maps.Directions.RouteMode.walking });

directionsManager.setRequestOptions({ routeMode: Microsoft.Maps.Directions.RouteMode.transit });
```

Traffic

If directions are one of the key map use cases, then checking traffic information is right up there with
it. Thankfully, Bing Maps also provides a REST Service that allows for quick and easy querying of traffic
information. If what you want is just to view the current traffic conditions, you can load a traffic module for
the map as follows:

```
var trafficLayer = new Microsoft.Maps.Traffic.TrafficLayer(map);
trafficLayer.show();
```

You will want to set the view of the map to center on the particular area of interest using map.setView().
In Listing 6-7, we show you the full listing for displaying traffic conditions of a given location, which we pass
to the view from the model.

Listing 6-7. Displaying traffic conditions on a map for a given location

```
@model IEnumerable<MvcBingMapTraffic.Models.GeoLocation>

@{
    ViewBag.Title = "Index";
}

<html>
<head>
    <title>Add/Show Traffic Layer</title>
    <meta http-equiv="Content-Type" content="text/html; charset=utf-8" />
    <script type="text/javascript" src="http://ecn.dev.virtualearth.net/mapcontrol/
    mapcontrol.ashx?v=7.0"></script>
    <script type="text/javascript">
        var map = null;
        function trafficModuleLoaded() {
            @{
                var latitude = Model.ElementAt(0).Location.Latitude;
                var longitude = Model.ElementAt(0).Location.Longitude;
                @:setMapView(@latitude, @longitude);
            }
        }
        function loadTrafficModule() {
            Microsoft.Maps.loadModule('Microsoft.Maps.Traffic', { callback:
            trafficModuleLoaded });
        }
        function setMapView(lat, lon) {
            map.setView({ zoom: 10, center: new Microsoft.Maps.Location(lat, lon) })
        }
```

```
        function getMap() {
            map = new Microsoft.Maps.Map(document.getElementById('myMap'), { credentials:
            'Your Bing Map Key' });
            loadTrafficModule();
        }
        function showTrafficLayer() {

            var trafficLayer = new Microsoft.Maps.Traffic.TrafficLayer(map);
            // show the traffic Layer
            trafficLayer.show();
        }
    </script>
</head>
<body onload="getMap();">
    <div id='myMap' style="position:relative; width:1000px; height:500px;"></div>
    <div>
        <input type="button" value="ShowTrafficLayer" onclick="showTrafficLayer();" />
    </div>
    <div id='output'> </div>
</body>
</html>
```

In Figure 6-5 we show you the traffic conditions around Union Square, San Francisco.

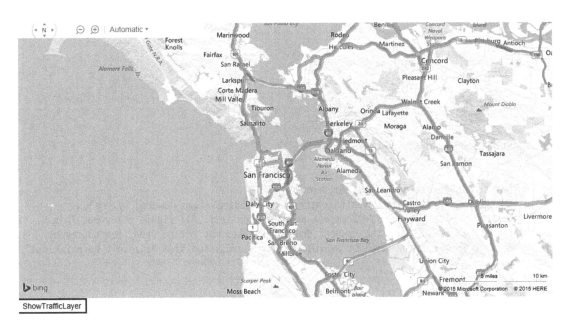

Figure 6-5. *Traffic conditions for a given location*

Sometimes you will want to get specific traffic incidents. For example, you may want to determine if there was a road accident or there is some construction. The Traffic REST API allows you to query for this information. A basic query will look like the following:

```
var trafficRequest = 'http://dev.virtualearth.net/REST/v1/Incidents/' + latitude1 + ','
+ longitude1 + ',' + latitude2 + ',' + longitude2 + '?key=' + credentials;
```

In this query, we have specified a bounding box for which we want the traffic incidents returned. Aside from the MapArea, there are a number of other optional fields that can be included in the query:

- **includeLocationCodes**: a Boolean parameter that defaults to false. It returns the location codes, which provide pre-defined road segment traffic information.

- **Severity**: Indicates the severity of the incident. The return value is from 1 (Low Impact) to 4 (Serious)

- **Type**: Specifies the type of traffic incident to return. There are 11 different types:

  - Accident

  - Congestion

  - Disabled vehicle

  - Mass transit

  - Miscellaneous

  - Other news

  - Planned event

  - Road hazard

  - Construction

  - Alert

  - Weather

A sample JSON response could be as follows:

```
{
    "authenticationResultCode":"ValidCredentials",
    "brandLogoUri":"http:\/\/dev.virtualearth.net\/Branding\/logo_powered_by.png",
    "copyright":"Copyright © 2011 Microsoft and its suppliers. All rights reserved. This
API cannot be accessed and the content and any results may not be used, reproduced or
transmitted in any manner without express written permission from Microsoft Corporation.",
    "resourceSets":[
        {
            "estimatedTotal":131,
            "resources":[
                {
                    "__type":"TrafficIncident:http:\/\/schemas.microsoft.com\/search\/local\/
                    ws\/rest\/v1",
                    "point":{
                        "type":"Point",
                        "coordinates":[
```

```
                    38.85135,
                    -94.34033
                ]
            },
            "congestion":"",
            "description":"MO-150 is closed between 5th Ave S and Court Dr -
            construction",
            "detour":"",
            "end":"\/Date(1310396400000)\/",
            "incidentId":210546697,
            "lane":"",
            "lastModified":"\/Date(1309391096593)\/",
            "roadClosed":true,
            "severity":3,
            "start":"\/Date(1307365200000)\/",
            "type":9,
            "verified":true
        },
        {
            "__type":"TrafficIncident:http:\/\/schemas.microsoft.com\/search\/local\/ws\/
            rest\/v1",
            "point":{
                "type":"Point",
                "coordinates":[
                    38.85872,
                    -94.54638
                ]
            },
            "congestion":"",
            "description":"Botts Rd is closed between Andrews Rd and 142nd St -
            construction",
            "detour":"To go north take US-71 NB to 140th St and go west on 140th St to access
            Botts Rd- To go south continue west on MO-150 to Thunderbird Rd to 149th St",
            "end":"\/Date(1315244760000)\/",
            "incidentId":191097424,
            "lane":"",
            "lastModified":"\/Date(1309391096593)\/",
            "roadClosed":true,
            "severity":1,
            "start":"\/Date(1295704800000)\/",
            "type":9,
            "verified":true
        }
        ]
    }
    ],
    "statusCode":200,
    "statusDescription":"OK",
    "traceId":"38491198bf6a42f5b7e60c18aa08ec02"
}
```

Alternatively, by specifying the output parameter to be (o=xml), you can receive an XML output instead.

Theming

You may want to apply the latest Bing Maps site designs to your own applications. For this, you will use the Theme module. As with the other modules, you will load the Theme module using the `loadModule()` command. We already showed you how you could add pushpins in Chapter 5, but, alternatively, you can add pushpins using the Theme module. In Listing 6-8, we show you how you can add a pushpin and infobox for a given location. The code places a pushpin in the given location and adds an information box containing the name of the point of interest. Again, we have used the same model and controller as all the other sample applications in this chapter have, so you will not be surprised by the pushpins being located at Union Square and Stanford University, shown in Figure 6-6. Upon hovering over one of the pushpins with the cursor, the infobox appears.

Listing 6-8. Theme module to add pushpins and infoboxes

```
@model IEnumerable<MvcBingMapTheming.Models.GeoLocation>

@{
    ViewBag.Title = "Index";
}


<!DOCTYPE HTML PUBLIC "-//W3C//DTD XHTML 1.0 Transitional//EN" "http://www.w3.org/TR/xhtml1/
DTD/xhtml1-transitional.dtd">
<html>
<head>
    <title>Load map with navigation bar module</title>
    <meta http-equiv="Content-Type" content="text/html; charset=utf-8" />
    <script type="text/javascript" src="http://ecn.dev.virtualearth.net/mapcontrol/
    mapcontrol.ashx?v=7.0"></script>
    <script type="text/javascript">
                var map = null;
                function getMap() {
                    Microsoft.Maps.loadModule('Microsoft.Maps.Themes.BingTheme', {
                        callback: function () {
                            map = new Microsoft.Maps.Map(document.
                            getElementById('myMap'),
                    {
                        credentials: 'Your Bing Map Key',
                        theme: new Microsoft.Maps.Themes.BingTheme()
                    });
                    GetLocationsAndAddPins();
                        }
                    });
                }
                function GetLocationsAndAddPins(){
            @foreach (var item in Model)
                    {
                        @:AddPins('@item.LocationName', @item.Location.Latitude, @item.
                        Location.Longitude);
                }
                 @{
                    var centerLat = Model.ElementAt(0).Location.Latitude;
```

```
                var centerLon = Model.ElementAt(0).Location.Longitude;
                @:CenterMap(@centerLat, @centerLon);
            }
          }

    function AddPins(locationName, lat, lon){
        var pin = new Microsoft.Maps.Pushpin(new Microsoft.Maps.Location(lat, lon),
        null);
        map.entities.push(pin);
        map.entities.push(new Microsoft.Maps.Infobox(new Microsoft.Maps.Location(lat,lon),
        { title: locationName, description: 'description here', pushpin: pin }));
    }

    function CenterMap(lat, lon){
        map.setView({ center: new Microsoft.Maps.Location(lat, lon), zoom: 9});
    }

    </script>
</head>
<body onload="getMap();">
    <div id='myMap' style="position:relative; width:1000px; height:500px;"></div>
</body>
</html>
```

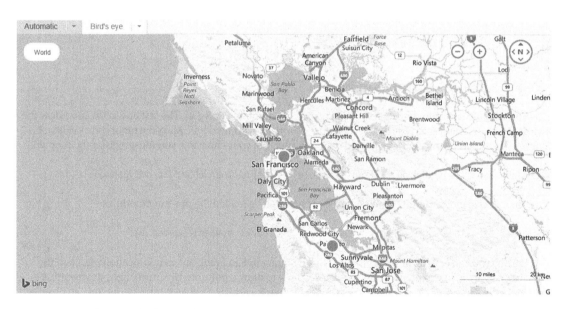

Figure 6-6. Pushpin and infobox added using the Theme module

111

Building Your Own Modules

Up until now, we have shown you how to use the out-of-the-box modules that Bing Maps AJAX Control has provided for you. One of the nice features of AJAX is that you can build your own module and include it in your web application.

The first thing you will want to do is to build the module itself. In Listing 6-9, we have written a simple Javascript module that takes four locations and draws a polygon, using those locations as the vertices.

Listing 6-9. Self-made module that draws a polygon for given locations

```
// polygonmodule.js

function PolygonModule(map)
{
    // Draw a polygon using the given locations as vertices
    this.drawPolygon = function(location0, location1, location2, location3)
        {
            // Initialize the polygon locations
            var points = new Array(5);
            points[0] = location0;
            points[1] = location1;
            points[2] = location2;
            points[3] = location3;
            points[4] = location0;
            var polyline = new Microsoft.Maps.Polyline(points, null);

            map.entities.push(polyline);
        }
}
Microsoft.Maps.moduleLoaded('PolygonModule');
```

This module has a function `drawPolygon` that draws the actual polygon. The last line in the module is the `Microsoft.Maps.moduleLoaded('PolygonModule')`, which is essential for calling the main code's callback function. This module must now be hosted on a web server of your choosing; you must register the module:

```
Microsoft.Maps.registerModule("PolygonModule", "http://YourWebServer/polygonmodule.js");
```

Then, you load the module much in the same way you've loaded the pre-built modules:

```
Microsoft.Maps.loadModule("PolygonModule", { callback: myModuleLoaded });
```

Finally, you can call the module. We use Union Square in San Francisco as our location, much in the same way as we did in Chapter 5 when you learned how to draw a polygon. Unsurprisingly, the resulting map looks the same as it did in Chapter 5, despite the use of a drawing polygon module, as you can observe in Figure 6-7. This example is somewhat silly, as it is abstracting a function that requires no abstraction, but we kept it simple so the code listing would be easy to follow. The full code for the view is in Listing 6-10.

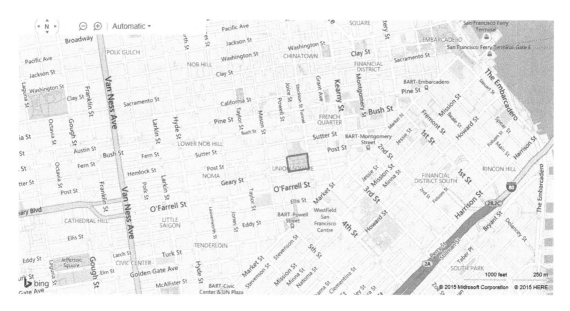

Figure 6-7. *Polygon drawn around Union Square using the polygon module from Listing 6-9*

Listing 6-10. Calling the custom module

```
<%@ Page Language="C#" Inherits="System.Web.Mvc.ViewPage<List<MvcBingMapsModules.Models.
GeoLocation>>" %>

<!DOCTYPE HTML PUBLIC "-//W3C//DTD XHTML 1.0 Transitional//EN"
        "http://www.w3.org/TR/xhtml1/DTD/xhtml1-transitional.dtd">
<html>
<head>
    <title></title>
    <meta http-equiv="Content-Type" content="text/html; charset=utf-8">

    <script type="text/javascript" src="http://ecn.dev.virtualearth.net/mapcontrol/
    mapcontrol.ashx?v=7.0"></script>

    <script type="text/javascript">

        var map;

        function myModuleLoaded() {
            var polygonModule = new PolygonModule(map);
            polygonModule.drawPolygon(new Microsoft.Maps.Location(37.788327, -122.408447),
                new Microsoft.Maps.Location(37.788531, -122.406837),
                new Microsoft.Maps.Location(37.787607, -122.406676),
                new Microsoft.Maps.Location(37.787412, -122.408264));

            map.setView({ zoom: 15, center: new Microsoft.Maps.Location(37.788327,
            -122.408447) })
        }
```

113

```
        function GetMap() {
            // Initialize the map
            var options = { credentials: 'Your Bing Map Key' };
            map = new Microsoft.Maps.Map(document.getElementById('mapDiv'), options);

            // Register and load the arrow module
            Microsoft.Maps.registerModule("PolygonModule", "http://YourWebServer/
            polygonmodule.js");
            Microsoft.Maps.loadModule("PolygonModule", { callback: myModuleLoaded });

        }

    </script>
</head>
<body onload="GetMap();">
    <div id='mapDiv' style="position:relative; width:1000px; height:500px;"></div>
</body>
</html>
```

Wrapping Up

In this chapter, you learned how to do more with Bing Maps for web-based applications. Routing, geolocating, and querying for traffic information have all become basic use cases for maps. We showed you how to do that using either the REST Services or the AJAX Control modules. The beauty of the modules is that Bing Maps allows you to build your own modules. In subsequent chapters, you will learn how to create Bing Maps applications for other platforms.

CHAPTER 7

■ ■ ■

Bing Maps for WPF

Web applications are well and good, but not every application is well suited to being a web application. Sometimes, what's called for is a plain, old-fashioned, double-clickable executable, because of either business or feature constraints. Location-enabling a .NET application isn't any more difficult than adding a Bing Maps assembly and control; in this chapter and the next, we will show you how to do this–first for Windows Presentation Foundation (WPF) here and then for Windows Universal applications in the following chapter.

In this chapter, we will show you the ins and outs of using Bing Maps in WPF applications. As you might imagine from Microsoft, it's as easy as adding an assembly to your project and writing a bit of XAML and code-behind to get started. You'll learn what the control is capable of, how to configure a project to include the control, and the basic organization of classes in the control. Then, we will dive into coding with the control, showing you first a simple "Hello Map" application followed by the WPF version of our earthquake application, and wrapping up with examples of how to use the two Bing Maps services that are part of Bing Maps but not the control: the geocoding and routing services. Note that WPF is now a little long in the tooth, and if you're developing an application from scratch, you may want to consider the more powerful Bing Maps control for Windows 10 for universal applications.

Introducing the Bing Maps for WPF Control

The features and design of the Bing Maps for WPF control will be pretty familiar to you if you studied our description of the web control, but there are some differences. Like the AJAX control for the web, the WPF control

- provides a rendering of the world in aerial, street, and hybrid (aerial plus roads) modes using raster tiles;

- supports free panning and zooming using traditional affordances (mouse, touch, scrollwheel, and pinch-to-zoom); and

- permits you to add layers that contain polygons, polylines, and map markers.

There are key differences, however. Most notably, with Bing Maps you construct your user interface around the map and its components using the Extensible Application Markup Language (XAML) you already know and love as a Windows developer. As you will see later in the chapter, you can even construct map markers in XAML. On the feature side, it largely has parity with the AJAX control, although as we write this, there's no support for traffic display.

Note   Like the AJAX control, the Bing Maps for WPF control requires a connection to the Internet to obtain its map tiles. You can use the control in your WPF application even if the computer running your application is not connected to the Internet, but it will not be able to download or render maps without an Internet connection!

Getting the Control

The Bing Maps for WPF control is made available as an assembly from the Microsoft Download Center; go to http://bit.ly/16xHcy1 or do a Bing search for "Bing Maps WPF Control," download the installer, and follow the installation instructions. It requires the .NET Framework 4.0 and the Windows SDK, both of which you should already have installed if you have a recent version of Microsoft Visual Studio installed. Applications built with the control run under Windows 7, Windows 8, Windows 8.1, and Windows 10, although if you're targeting only Windows 10, you should use the new Bing Maps control that's part of Windows 10—see the next two chapters for details.

Just as with the AJAX control, you'll need a Bing Maps key. If you skipped getting one when you read Chapter 2, now's your chance. Follow the steps there, registering for a Windows Live ID if you don't have one and then getting a Bing Maps Basic API Key. You can prototype your application without one, but you'll get a big nasty message every time you display a map about how you need an API key, so it's easier just to get one, especially before you show your application to anyone else.

Once you get the control SDK installed, you'll need to add a reference to its assembly in your WPF application. Doing this is the same as adding any other assembly:

1.   Select the solution you'd like to add the reference to.

2.   Right-click and choose Add Reference.

3.   In the dialog that appears, click Browse on the left and then press the Browse button.

4.   Navigate to the directory where the Bing Maps for WPF Control assembly is (by default, you should find it in C:\Program Files (x86)\Bing Maps WPF Control\V1\Libraries).

Key Classes and Relationships

The Bing Maps for WPF assembly has four namespaces you need to use in your application:

- The Microsoft.Maps.MapControl.WPF namespace, which contains the workhorse classes you're likely to use the most when you use the control, like Map and MapLayer.

- The Microsoft.Maps.MapControl.WPF.Core namespace has fundamental classes like exceptions and enumerations that are used in the implementation of the control.

- The Microsoft.Maps.MapControl.WPF.Design namespace is ill-named in our opinion, because it doesn't have anything to do with design per se, and instead contains classes for parsing and data-type conversion.

- The Microsoft.Maps.MapControl.WPF.Overlays namespace contains the implementation of default overlays you may want to place on a map, like the compass overlay or the scale control that shows the map scale.

When you use the control, you'll usually start by instantiating one or more instances of Map (in Microsoft.Maps.MapControl.WPF), configuring it and wiring some event handlers to it, and possibly configuring one or more overlays with data to overlay on the map.

Two key properties you need to be aware that the Map control has are the CredentialProvider and the Mode properties. Specify your API key as the value of the CredentialProvider attribute; failing to do this lets the Map control load, but not without a note across the front saying you need to include the API key. The Mode attribute lets you pick what kind of data the Map control displays, of the following:

- Road: Shows the street network in a symbolic mode

- Aerial: Shows an aerial view from the nadir perspective

- AerialWithLabels: Shows an aerial view from the nadir perspective and includes road labels as you zoom in

Map inherits from MapCore, which is where you'll find most of the methods you expect for a Map control, including:

- The Center property, which you can set or get to determine the map's geographic center. The value of this property is an instance of the Location lass, which bears the latitude and longitude of the location.

- The ZoomLevel property, which you can set or get to determine the current zoom level of the map. Higher values indicate more zoom; a ZoomLevel of 1 shows the whole world, while approximately 10 shows city-level detail, and approximately 20 is the highest level of detail you can presently render.

The MapCore class also has the very handy TryLocationToViewportPoint and TryViewportPointToLocation methods, which are to be used when you need to convert between a latitude and longitude and the corresponding view point on the map. It also has a number of SetView methods, which let you center the map on a point with a specific zoom level, or indicate that a specific geographic rectangle should be shown (at which point the control determines the appropriate center coordinate and zoom level to ensure that the rectangle you specify is in view).

Events generated by the Map control are split between the MapCore and Map classes; as you might imagine, the usual bevy of user events for things like key, touch, and mouse events. There are some specific events you may want to watch for, however:

- The ModeChanged event, which occurs when the map mode (aerial, road, or both) changes

- The ViewChangeStart and ViewChangeEnd events, which occur at the beginning and end of animated transitions, respectively. (There's also a ViewChangeOnFrame event, if you want to synchronize something to animation frame display. Of course, any processing you do in this event should be fast, or you run the risk of dropping animation frames.)

As those events suggest, the Map control includes animation when transitioning from one position to another. Generally, that's something you want; animation between the current viewpoint and a new viewpoint gives the user something to look at while the data loads, and provides some orientation to the user as well. The Map class has a property, AnimationLevel, which can be set to one of the following values:

- Full, indicating that animation should happen both when properties are mutated and as a result of user input

- None, indicating that no animation should occur

- UserInput, indicating that animation should occur only as a result of user input

Bing Maps gives you a few custom layers called *overlays*; these overlays let you show and hide

- the map compass, indicating which way is north (the Compass class);
- the copyright information for the map (the Copyright class);
- the Bing logo (the Logo class); and
- the map scale (using the Scale class).

Like the AJAX version of the control, additional information for the Map control is organized to display in layers. The assembly provides the MapLayer class, a class that positions its child elements using geographic, rather than viewpoint, coordinates. MapLayer instances are glorified Panel instances; most of the class's interface relates to child management, or the bookkeeping necessary to map between map geocoordinates and view coordinates. Odds are you'll make one or more MapLayer instances and add child objects to it, and then show or hide those layers to make your map data visible or invisible.

Map pushpins let you mark individual points on the map. They have a Location property, which lets you specify the location of a pushpin on the map in geocoordinates, as well as a heading, which indicates how the pushpin should be rotated. They're full citizens of the WPF world, meaning that they can generate all the events an interactive control can (touch, stylus, mouse, and keyboard), and can have a Template property that indicates what the pushpin should look like (the default is an orange circle with a stem). You can also plot lines and polygons on the map using the MapPolyline and MapPolygon classes; these use Location instances for their points.

Using the Control

Enough generalities—let's dig in and write some code using the Bing Maps control. We will begin with a simple example to show you how to display a map and process events from the map, and then move on from there to our sample application, and close our discussion with an example that ties together the Bing Maps control with the Bing Maps services for geocoding and routing.

Kicking the Tires

Let's begin with a "Hello Map"–style application. Open Visual Studio and do the following:

1. Create a new C# WPF application. We called ours "WPFHelloMap."

2. Add a reference to the Bing Maps for WPF assembly. Right-click the project, choose Add Reference, and navigate to Microsoft.Maps.MapControl.WPF.dll.

3. Add a namespace for the Bing Maps assembly and add your Bing Maps API key as a resource to your App.xaml file. It should look something like this:

```
<Application x:Class="WPFHelloMap.App"
  xmlns="http://schemas.microsoft.com/winfx/2006/xaml/presentation"
  xmlns:x="http://schemas.microsoft.com/winfx/2006/xaml"
  xmlns:map="clr-namespace:Microsoft.Maps.MapControl.WPF;
assembly=Microsoft.Maps.MapControl.WPF"
  StartupUri="MainWindow.xaml">
  <Application.Resources>
    <map:ApplicationIdCredentialsProvider
      x:Key="MyCredentials"
      ApplicationId="your-id" />
  </Application.Resources>
</Application>
```

4. Open the `MainWindow.xaml` file, add a namespace for the assembly, and add an instance of the Map class. While you're at it, you might want to make the window a little bigger:

```
<Window x:Class="WPFHelloMap.MainWindow"
  xmlns="http://schemas.microsoft.com/winfx/2006/xaml/presentation"
  xmlns:x="http://schemas.microsoft.com/winfx/2006/xaml"
  xmlns:map="clr-namespace:Microsoft.Maps.MapControl.WPF;
  assembly=Microsoft.Maps.MapControl.WPF"
  Title="MainWindow" Height="600" Width="800">
  <Grid>
    <map:Map
      x:Name="Map"
      Mode="AerialWithLabels"
      HorizontalAlignment="Stretch"
      VerticalAlignment="Stretch"
      AnimationLevel="Full"
      CredentialsProvider="{StaticResource MyCredentials}" >
    </map:Map>
  </Grid>
</Window>
```

5. Run the application. You should be rewarded with a window containing an aerial map of the world, as you see in Figure 7-1. Try panning and zooming the map with your mouse (or finger, if you're running Windows 8 on a touch-enabled device).

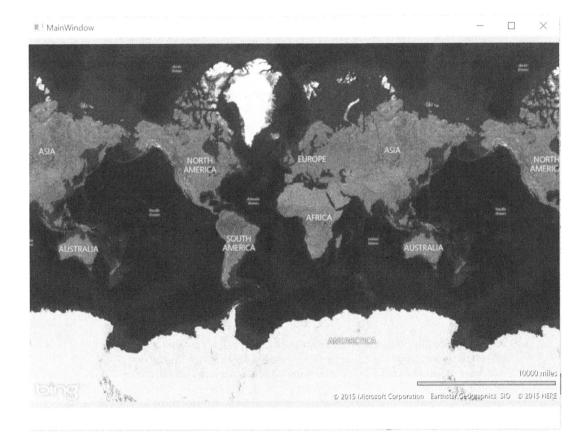

Figure 7-1. *Hello world, aerial style!*

This is just basic XAML; let's do a bit more XAML hacking and add a button that centers the map on one of our favorite coffee shops.

1. Add a button someplace to the XAML and wire up a click handler for it. You can just slap down a button over the map with the code here, or do something fancier with a Grid layout (which we did, as you can see from the next figure).

```
<Button Height="32" Width="128" Content="Show Red Rock" Click="Button_Clicked"/>
```

2. Add some XAML for a pushpin inside the map:Map tag:

```
<map:Map
  x:Name="Map"
  Mode="AerialWithLabels"
  HorizontalAlignment="Stretch"
  VerticalAlignment="Stretch"
  AnimationLevel="Full"
    CredentialsProvider="{StaticResource MyCredentials}" >
    <map:Pushpin
      Location="37.39366,-122.07888"/>
</map:Map>
```

3. Add the following to the code-behind in `MainWindow.xaml.cs`. Make sure you include the `using` directive at the top of the code-behind:

```
using Microsoft.Maps.MapControl.WPF;
...
public void Button_Clicked(object sender, RoutedEventArgs e)
{
  Location redrock = new Location(37.39366,-122.07888);
  Map.SetView(redrock, 20);
}
```

4. Run the app and push the button. You'll see a short animation to Red Rock in Mountain View (Figure 7-2).

Figure 7-2. A pushpin on the map

Finally, let's hook up an event handler that shows your latitude and longitude wherever you click.

1. Add the event bindings to your XAML:

```
<map:Map Grid.Row="0"
  x:Name="Map"
  Mode="AerialWithLabels"
  HorizontalAlignment="Stretch"
  VerticalAlignment="Stretch"
  AnimationLevel="Full"
  MouseUp="Map_MouseUp"
  CredentialsProvider="{StaticResource MyCredentials}" >
```

2. Add the code-behind for the event to show a message box:

```
private void Map_MouseUp(object sender, MouseButtonEventArgs e)
{
  Location ll = Map.ViewportPointToLocation(e.GetPosition(Map));
  MessageBox.Show(ll.Latitude + "," + ll.Longitude);
}
```

Try it out and see! (Figure 7-3)

Figure 7-3. Click handling

Earthquakes Everywhere!

Let's take a look at a more involved sample, our earthquake application, which you can see in Figure 7-4. Most of the interesting code is in the XAML, so let's look at that first, in Listing 7-1.

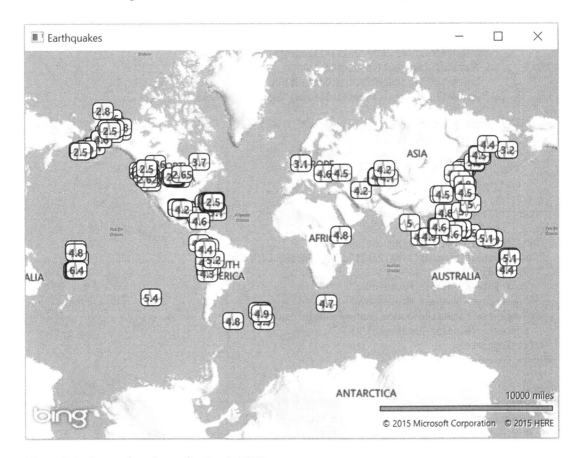

Figure 7-4. *Our earthquake application in WPF*

Listing 7-1. The MainWindow.xaml for the earthquake application

```xml
<Window x:Class="WPFMapApplication.MainWindow"
  xmlns="http://schemas.microsoft.com/winfx/2006/xaml/presentation"
  xmlns:x="http://schemas.microsoft.com/winfx/2006/xaml"
  xmlns:map="clr-namespace:Microsoft.Maps.MapControl.WPF;
assembly=Microsoft.Maps.MapControl.WPF"
  Title="Earthquakes" Height="480" Width="640">

<Window.Resources>
  <BitmapImage x:Key="EarthquakeIcon" UriSource="Resources/icon.png" />
  <ControlTemplate x:Key="CustomPushpinTemplate" TargetType="map:Pushpin">
    <Grid x:Name="ContentGrid"
          HorizontalAlignment="Center"
          VerticalAlignment="Center">
```

123

```xml
        <StackPanel>
          <Grid Margin="0" Width="25" Height="20">
           <Rectangle Fill="White"
             Stroke="#FF000000"
             RadiusX="5" RadiusY="5"/>
           <Image Source="Resources/icon.png"
             Width="25" Height="20" Opacity="0.25" />
             <ContentPresenter HorizontalAlignment="Center"
               VerticalAlignment="Center"
               Content="{TemplateBinding Content}"
               ContentTemplate="{TemplateBinding ContentTemplate}"
               Margin="0"
               TextBlock.FontFamily="Segoe UI"
               TextBlock.FontWeight="Bold"
               TextBlock.Foreground="#FFB8000B"/>
          </Grid>
        </StackPanel>
      </Grid>
   </ControlTemplate>

   <DataTemplate x:Key="EarthquakeTemplate">
     <map:Pushpin map:MapLayer.Position="{Binding Location}"
      Tag="{Binding}"
      MouseEnter="Pushpin_MouseEnter"
      MouseLeave="Pushpin_MouseLeave"
      Template="{StaticResource CustomPushpinTemplate}"
      Content="{Binding Magnitude}"/>
   </DataTemplate>
</Window.Resources>

<Grid>
  <map:Map x:Name="DisplayMap"
    CredentialsProvider="{StaticResource MyCredentials}">
     <map:Map.Children>
       <map:MapItemsControl
         ItemsSource="{Binding Earthquakes}"
         ItemTemplate="{StaticResource EarthquakeTemplate}"/>

       <map:MapLayer x:Name="ContentPopupLayer">
         <Grid x:Name="ContentPopup"
           Visibility="Collapsed"
           Background="White"
           Opacity="0.85">
           <StackPanel Margin="15">
             <TextBlock x:Name="ContentPopupText"
               FontSize="12"
               FontWeight="Bold"/>
             <TextBlock x:Name="ContentPopupDescription"
               FontSize="12"/>
           </StackPanel>
         </Grid>
```

```
        </map:MapLayer>
      </map:Map.Children>
    </map:Map>
  </Grid>
</Window>
```

First up is a `ControlTemplate` for the custom pushpin we use to mark the location of each earthquake.

Next is a `DataTemplate`, which encapsulates the pushpin itself. It maps the `Content` of the pushpin to the earthquake's magnitude (we'll show you the model and `Earthquake` class later) and assigns a couple of event handlers so we can show more detail about the earthquake when hovering over the pushpin.

The map itself in the `Grid` view is straightforward, but this is the first time we've shown you a `MapItemControl`. It's a class that lets you use a `MapLayer` as an `ItemsPanel`—essential if you want to bind data to an `ItemSource` and `ItemTemplate`, which is what we do here. The template is our `DataTemplate` containing our custom `Pushpin`, and the data behind the binding will be our list of earthquakes.

Finally, we use a custom `MapLayer` to wrap a `StackPanel` that will show the earthquake's magnitude and date/timestamp when you hover over a pushpin. We use a `MapLayer` here, rather than a conventional layer, because we want to position the text legend in geographic space, rather than the pixel space of the control (so that the legend hovers near the earthquake event with a minimum of coding on our part to achieve this).

The code-behind for the XAML is straightforward (we've eliminated `using` directives and the namespace for brevity); it's shown in Listing 7-2.

Listing 7-2. The code-behind for Earthquake's user interface

```
public partial class MainWindow : Window
{
  public MainWindow()
  {
    InitializeComponent();
    DataContext = new EarthquakeViewModel();
  }

  private void Pushpin_MouseEnter(object sender, MouseEventArgs e)
  {
    FrameworkElement pin = sender as FrameworkElement;
    MapLayer.SetPosition(ContentPopup, MapLayer.GetPosition(pin));
    MapLayer.SetPositionOffset(ContentPopup, new Point(20, -20));

    var quake = (Earthquake)pin.Tag;

    ContentPopupText.Text = "Magnitude " + quake.Magnitude;
    ContentPopupDescription.Text = quake.When.ToString();
    ContentPopup.Visibility = Visibility.Visible;
  }

  private void Pushpin_MouseLeave(object sender, MouseEventArgs e)
  {
    ContentPopup.Visibility = Visibility.Collapsed;
  }
}
```

Our constructor needs to configure the DataContext with our data model.

The MouseEnter handler for the pushpin must figure out where to position the context popup that will contain the earthquake information details; it does this by getting the position of the pin generating the event and setting the ContentPopup's position to that pin, offset by a small amount. It then reads the data associated with that pin (an Earthquake object) and populates the context popup with the data before setting the popup's visibility to show the popup. The MouseLeave handler just flips the visibility, hiding the popup.

The Earthquake class (Listing 7-3) is a straight-up data container class, and needs no further explanation.

Listing 7-3. The Earthquake class

```
public class Earthquake
{
  public string Title { get; set; }
  public string Description { get; set; }
  public double Magnitude { get; set; }
  public Location Location { get; set; }
  public DateTime When { get; set; }
  public Earthquake(Location where,
                    DateTime when,
                    double magnitude,
                    string title,
                    string description = "")
  {
    Location = where;
    When = when;
    Magnitude = magnitude;
    Title = title;
    Description = description;
  }
}
```

The associated model is equally simple (Listing 7-4).

Listng 7-4. The EarthquakeViewModel class

```
public class EarthquakeViewModel : INotifyPropertyChanged
{
  private ObservableCollection<Earthquake> _earthquakes;
  public ObservableCollection<Earthquake> Earthquakes
  {
    get { return _earthquakes; }
    set
    {
      _earthquakes = value;
      OnPropertyChanged("Earthquakes");
    }
  }
```

```
public EarthquakeViewModel()
{
  USGSEarthquakeService.GetRecentEarthquakes((o, ea) =>
  {
    Earthquakes = new ObservableCollection<Earthquake>(ea.Locations);
  });
}

public event PropertyChangedEventHandler PropertyChanged;
protected virtual void OnPropertyChanged(string propertyName)
{
  if (PropertyChanged != null)
    PropertyChanged(this, new PropertyChangedEventArgs(propertyName));
}
}
```

The only interesting thing going on here is in the constructor, where we populate the model from our USGS Earthquake service, which is backed by the WCF service you saw us write in Chapter 4.

Geocoding with the Bing Maps Geocoder Service

Although not formally part of the Bing Maps control, the Bing Maps Geocoder service lets you determine the latitude and longitude of an address, or to map the nearest address to a given latitude and longitude. It's a prerequisite for things like routing, in which your users are likely thinking in terms of addresses and the service is thinking in terms of geocoordinates. Using the Bing Maps Geocoder Service is just like using any other SOAP service. You need to add a service reference to the geocoding service at `http://dev.virtualearth.net/webservices/v1/geocodeservice/geocodeservice.svc`. The resulting interface, IGeocodeService, has four methods:

- Geocode, which takes an address request and determines its geolocation

- GeocodeAsync, an asynchronous version of Geocode

- ReverseGeocode, which takes a position and determines its approximate address

- ReverseGeocodeAsync, an asynchronous version of ReverseGeocode

These take a GeocodeRequest, which has fields for things like the address and position of a location.

■ **Note** The Bing Maps Geocoder Service is part of the older Bing Maps SOAP interface, and is very easy to use in C# and .NET applications. If you're looking for a more modern REST interface to this service for things like web applications, be sure to check out the description of the Bing Maps REST API in Chapter 9.

Listing 7-5 shows how to perform a simple geocoding request.

Listing 7-5. Geocoding an address

```
BingGeocodeService.GeocodeResult result = null;

using (BingGeocodeService.GeocodeServiceClient client =
  new BingGeocodeService.GeocodeServiceClient("CustomBinding_IGeocodeService"))
{
  BingGeocodeService.GeocodeRequest request =
    new BingGeocodeService.GeocodeRequest();
  request.Credentials = new Credentials()
  {
    ApplicationId = (App.Current.Resources["MyCredentials"] as
      ApplicationIdCredentialsProvider).ApplicationId
  };
  request.Query = address;
  result = client.Geocode(request).Results[0];
}
return result;
```

Please note that you must provide your Bing API key as the request `Credentials`. The result structure includes the following fields:

- `Address` contains the address of the resulting reverse-geocode, if one was found, or the original address for a geocoding operation.

- `Locations` contains the latitude and longitude of the location.

- `Confidence` indicates the geocoder's confidence in the result.

We'll use the geocoder in the next section, when we route between two locations.

Routing with the Bing Maps Routing Service

Our final example shows how to compute a route with the Bing Maps Routing Service, another SOAP service hosted by Microsoft. As you can see in Figure 7-5, it plots a route from downtown Sunnyvale to the café that so occupied our maps at the beginning of the chapter, Red Rock Coffee.

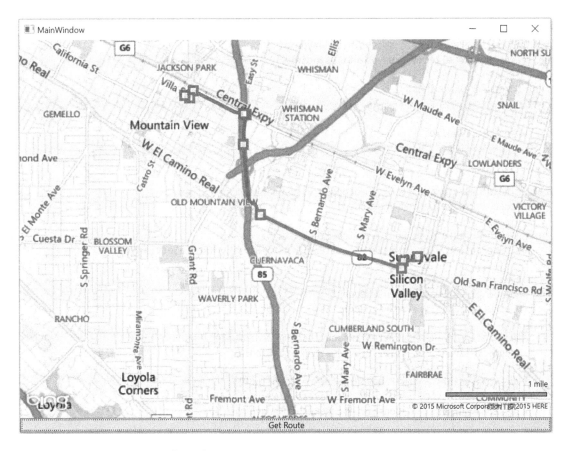

Figure 7-5. *The routing example application*

To use the Bing Maps Routing Service, you'll need to add the service endpoint to your application. It's found at `http://dev.virtualearth.net/webservices/v1/routeservice/routeservice.svc`.

■ **Note**   The Bing Maps Routing Service is part of the older Bing Maps SOAP interface, and is very easy to use in C# and .NET applications. If you're looking for a more modern REST interface to this service for things like Web applications, be sure to check out the description of the Bing Maps REST API in Chapter 9.

Our routing is done in our view model, which geocodes the source and destination positions, calculates a route, and then converts the route to a `MapPolyline` that we show on the map. Listing 7-6 shows the relevant parts of the view model.

Listing 7-6. Determining a route and populating the data model's Waypoints field

```
private ObservableCollection<Waypoint> _waypoints;
public ObservableCollection<Waypoint> Waypoints
{
  get { return _waypoints; }
  set
  {
    _waypoints = value;
    OnPropertyChanged("Waypoints");
  }
}
private void CalculateRoute(BingGeocodeService.GeocodeResult from,
  BingGeocodeService.GeocodeResult to)
{
  using (BingRouteService.RouteServiceClient client =
    new BingRouteService.RouteServiceClient("CustomBinding_IRouteService"))
  {
    BingRouteService.RouteRequest request =
      new BingRouteService.RouteRequest();
    request.Credentials = new Credentials()
    {
      ApplicationId = (App.Current.Resources["MyCredentials"] as
        ApplicationIdCredentialsProvider).ApplicationId
    };
    request.Waypoints = new BingRouteService.Waypoint[2];
    request.Waypoints[0] = ConvertGeocodeResultToWaypoint(from);
    request.Waypoints[1] = ConvertGeocodeResultToWaypoint(to);

    request.Options = new BingRouteService.RouteOptions();
    request.Options.RoutePathType = BingRouteService.RoutePathType.Points;

    RouteResult = client.CalculateRoute(request).Result;
  }

  Waypoints = new ObservableCollection<Waypoint>();

  foreach (BingRouteService.ItineraryItem item
    in RouteResult.Legs[0].Itinerary)
  {
    Waypoints.Add(new Waypoint()
      {
        Description = GetDirectionText(item),
        Location = new Location(item.Location.Latitude,
          item.Location.Longitude)
      });
  }
}
```

The Routing Service takes an array of waypoints along a route (so multi-stop routing is possible) and options such as whether the route should be for cars or pedestrians, and returns a list of `ItineraryItem` objects, one for each leg of the route. The `ItineraryItem` class has several fields about decision points along the route, including:

- The compass direction at the decision point to take

- The location of the decision point (which we use here as the vertexes of our geographic polyline)

- The description of the maneuver to be made at the decision point

- Warnings about the maneuver

In this example, we just stash the location of the decision point and the text for the maneuver in a container class, which we use to populate our polyline. The XAML uses the data from the model to show turn-by-turn directions at each decision point; when the model changes, we update the route line on the map by throwing away the old route line and creating a new one (Listing 7-7).

Listng 7-7. Creating a `MapPolyline` from the route

```
private static void OnRouteResultChanged(Map map,
  BingRouteService.RouteResult oldValue,
  BingRouteService.RouteResult newValue)
{
  MapPolyline line = new MapPolyline();
  line.Locations = new LocationCollection();
  line.Opacity = 0.80;
  line.Stroke = new SolidColorBrush(Colors.Magenta);
  line.StrokeThickness = 5.0;

  foreach (BingRouteService.Location l in newValue.RoutePath.Points)
  {
    line.Locations.Add(new Location(l.Latitude, l.Longitude));
  }

  var layer = GetRouteLineLayer(map);
  if (layer == null)
  {
    layer = new MapLayer();
    SetRouteLineLayer(map, layer);
  }

  layer.Children.Clear();
  layer.Children.Add(routeLine);

  LocationRect rect = new LocationRect(
    routeLine.Locations[0],
    routeLine.Locations[routeLine.Locations.Count - 1]);
  map.SetView(rect);
}
```

This code just creates a new polyline from the points along the route and adds it as the sole child of a `MapLayer` to contain the route line. (As you can see from this and the prior code, a lot of the code you need to write when working with the Bing Map SOAP services is just interconversion code to get from the service-layer classes to the appropriate Bing Maps classes, and vice versa.)

The XAML simply ties together the model, the map, and the layers for the polyline and the decision-point text box.

Wrapping Up

In this chapter, we've walked you through the basics of getting the Bing Maps for WPF control integrated with your WPF application as well as how to use it along with the Bing Maps SOAP services in a C# application.

The control itself is a full participant in WPF, handling the map-tile fetching, rendering, and generating of app-level events for user and map actions such as touch, mouse, and keyboard. As with other WPF controls, you can express most of your user interface in XAML, saving C# code for the code-behind that both handles events and provides a data model to the map so as to indicate what to display.

Microsoft also provides two SOAP services that are available to your application with your API key—one for geocoding and one for routing. You can use these as part of your location-aware applications, either in conjunction with map display or as separate components that add location-aware features for your own purposes.

■ ■ ■

Bing Maps for Windows Universal Applications

In Windows 10, Microsoft has introduced Windows Universal applications, which function on any platform running Windows 10, including desktops and tablets, as well as Windows Phones and Xbox One. By writing a Windows Universal application, you can target every platform running Windows 10—and there are a lot of them! As part of the Windows 10 platform, Microsoft includes a map feature that supports all the use cases you've come to expect, and a few more besides.

In this chapter, we will show you the support that Bing Maps brings to Windows Universal applications. If you have read the previous chapters that covered the various Bing Maps control interfaces, there's a lot here that should be familiar to you. However, there are some new capabilities that you'll want to take advantage of that are different from the Bing Maps for WPF control, and a lot of new features as well. You'll learn how to use the control to show basic maps, as well as how to use the new Aerial3D and Streetside features on devices that support those modes.

Introducing Bing Maps for Windows Universal Applications

If you've read any of the previous chapters on the various Bing Maps controls for different platforms, you're already starting to get the idea. For Windows Universal apps, the Bing Maps control supports viewing maps in either symbolic or aerial mode, with support for adding your own layers, pushpins, and shapes (filled and hollow). In addition, the version for Windows Store also includes:

- A new mode called Aerial 3D that shows an aerial 3D flyover of the region you're interested in, with or without having the road draped on the view.

- A new mode called Streetside that shows a streetview panorama around any point where Microsoft has collected imagery.

The Bing Maps for Windows Universal applications is included as part of Windows 10.

The software development kit (SDK) contains classes in the namespace `Windows.UI.Xaml.Controls.Maps` at `http://bit.ly/1MWfCOs`. The organization of the `Windows.UI.Xaml.Controls.Maps` namespace is similar to that of the namespace for the Bing Maps WPF control and mirrors somewhat the interfaces you get when you use the Bing Maps AJAX control, as well. It contains classes that represent a map, layers on a map, pushpins, and map shapes. As you might imagine, there's a host of supporting classes too, for things like events.

At the heart of the namespace is the Map class, which represents a map control on the screen. It's a subclass of Control, and has the usual properties you'd expect, including:

- Center, a Location that indicates the center of the map;

- MapServiceToken, which must contain your Bing Maps API key when you instantiate the control;

- Heading, the directional heading of the map in geometric degrees (0° corresponding to true north, 90° being east, and so forth);

- Style, one of MapType.Aerial, MapType.Aerial3D, MapType.Aerial3DWithRoads, MapType.AerialWithRoads, MapType.None, MapType.Roads, or MapType.Terrain, indicating the map's type;

- MinZoomLevel and MaxZoomLevel, indicating the minimum and maximum amount that a map can be zoomed;

- MinHeight and MaxHeight, indicating the minimum and maximum elevation for the camera viewing the map;

- ZoomLevel, the current map's zoom level;

- Height, the current camera elevation in meters;

- IsStreetsideSupported and Is3DSupported, indicating whether the Streetside and 3D modes are supported, respectively; and

- Pitch, the degree to which the map is pitched relative to the camera.

The map control supports animated transitions, so you'll probably want to set the various properties through the public methods that are available. There are two ways to set the orientation of the map—one focused on the old zoom level and center point you're used to from working with 2D maps, and a second involving the map scene that lets you specify the position of the camera viewing the map. Both of these are asynchronous methods, because they perform animation to orient the user as to where the viewer is being positioned.

For the first method, you can use the TrySetViewAsync method, which has overloads that take a center Geopoint, as well as one that takes the center Geopoint and the zoom level, heading, and pitch for the map. There's also TrySetViewBoundsAsync, which takes a region and a margin and attempts to position the camera so that the entire region you pass is visible within the margin you choose.

The camera approach that takes a MapScene is the one you should generally use for your applications, because it gives greater flexibility in positioning the camera over the map. You can use the static methods of MapScene class to get a copy of the current map scene by using MapScene.CreateFromCamera (handy when you're implementing the application back stack and need to remember how the user has oriented the map view), or you can create a map scene given initial conditions—such as a bounding box or a location, heading, and pitch—using MapScene.CreateFromBoundingBox or MapScene.CreateFromLocation. Once you have a MapScene in hand, you can use it to position the camera using TrySetSceneAsync. You can pass just a scene to obtain the new view using the default animation, or pass a specific map animation kind by passing one of the following: MapAnimationKind.Default, MapAnimationKind.None, MapAnimationKind.Bow, or MapAnimationKind.Linear.

The map generates a number of custom events that have to do with its underlying functionality, including events indicating when the map style changes, the target view changes, all of the map tiles have downloaded, events for each frame of an animation, and when an animation completes. There are user-interface events for taps, double taps, key down and up events, pointer movement, and scroll-wheel movement.

To encapsulate a hierarchy of objects on the map, the SDK provides the MapElement class, stored in a map's MapElements property, which lets you position objects on the map in geographic space. You can either create instances of MapElement and work with them directly—often in XAML—or add the object directly to the map's MapElements collection.

An obvious thing you can add to the map are MapIcon instances; by default, these are small icons that can have a text label or image and are just about the right size for touching with a simple numeric label and nothing else.

Finally, the namespace provides the StreetsidePanorama and StreetsideExperience classes. You use the StreetsidePanorama class to search for Streetside panorama positions around a given point, and then instantiate a StreetsideExperience class instance and pass it to the map control's CustomExperience property to show a street-level panorama that you can pan around and zoom.

Seeing the Map Control in Action

In the sections that follow, we will show you how to start using the control, handle events from the control, set the various map modes, and use Streetside.

Before you begin, be sure that you've registered for a Bing Maps API key (as we show you how to do in Chapter 2).

Your First Windows Universal Map App

Beginning at the beginning, Listing 8-1 shows the XAML for a simple Windows Universal application that displays a map control. We created this by:

1. Creating an empty Windows Universal application in C# in Visual Studio (File ➤ New Project... ➤ Visual C# ➤ Windows ➤ Universal ➤ Blank App (Universal Windows)), naming the application MapExample.

2. Putting the code you see in Listing 8-1 into the MainPage.xaml file, replacing the text "your-api-key" with your Bing Maps API key.

Listing 8-1. The simplest Windows Store map-enabled application

```
<Page
    x:Class="MapExample_1.MainPage"
    xmlns="http://schemas.microsoft.com/winfx/2006/xaml/presentation"
    xmlns:x="http://schemas.microsoft.com/winfx/2006/xaml"
    xmlns:local="using:MapExample_1"
    xmlns:d="http://schemas.microsoft.com/expression/blend/2008"
    xmlns:mc="http://schemas.openxmlformats.org/markup-compatibility/2006"
    xmlns:maps="using:Windows.UI.Xaml.Controls.Maps"
    mc:Ignorable="d">

    <Grid Background="{ThemeResource ApplicationPageBackgroundThemeBrush}">
        <maps:MapControl x:Name="map"
                        MapServiceToken ="your-api-key"/>
    </Grid>
</Page>
```

There are two things to pay attention to in this XAML: the namespace declaration for xmlns:maps in the Page declaration, and the maps:MapControl control instance in the grid.

135

This application code is enough to give you the basic map and venue-map navigation most applications start out with; it will look something similar to what you see in Figure 8-1.

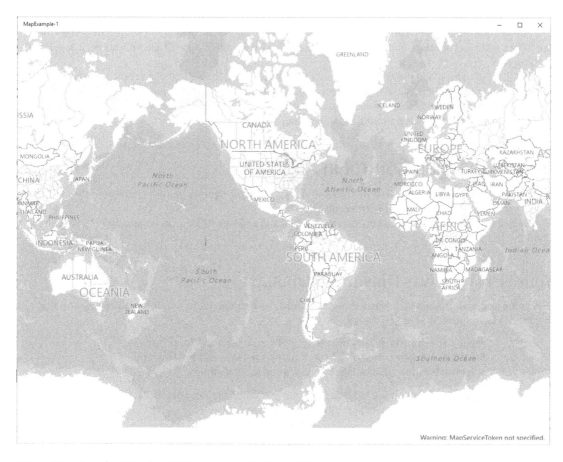

Figure 8-1. *Your first Windows 8 Universal application with a map*

You can interact with the map just as you would with the Windows 10 Map app. Try dragging to pan, use the scroll wheel or pinch to zoom, and right-click-drag to adjust the tilt of the map.

Creating a Custom Map Icon

Let's search the map for a location and place the location on the map. To do this, we'll use another new interface in Windows 10, the `MapLocationFinder` geocoder interface in `Windows.Devices.Geolocation`. Add a simple button bar to your XAML, as you see in Listing 8-2.

Listing 8-2. Adding a button bar and button to your application

```
<Page
    x:Class="MapExample_1.MainPage"
    xmlns="http://schemas.microsoft.com/winfx/2006/xaml/presentation"
    xmlns:x="http://schemas.microsoft.com/winfx/2006/xaml"
    xmlns:local="using:MapExample_1"
    xmlns:d="http://schemas.microsoft.com/expression/blend/2008"
    xmlns:mc="http://schemas.openxmlformats.org/markup-compatibility/2006"
    xmlns:maps="using:Windows.UI.Xaml.Controls.Maps"
    mc:Ignorable="d">
    <Grid Background="{ThemeResource ApplicationPageBackgroundThemeBrush}">
        <Grid.RowDefinitions>
            <RowDefinition Height="40"/>
            <RowDefinition Height="*"/>
        </Grid.RowDefinitions>
        <StackPanel Orientation="Horizontal">
            <Button x:Name="coffeeButton" Content="Coffee" Margin="3"
             Click="coffeeButton_Click"/>
        </StackPanel>
        <maps:MapControl x:Name="map" Grid.Row="1"
                         MapServiceToken ="your-api-key" />
    </Grid>
</Page>
```

Listing 8-3 shows the code for the `coffeeButton_Click` handler, which we insert in the main class of MainPage.xaml.cs.

Listing 8-3. The coffee button search handler

```
using System;
using System.Collections.Generic;
using System.IO;
using System.Linq;
using System.Runtime.InteropServices.WindowsRuntime;
using Windows.Foundation;
using Windows.Foundation.Collections;
using Windows.UI.Xaml;
using Windows.UI.Xaml.Controls;
using Windows.UI.Xaml.Controls.Primitives;
using Windows.UI.Xaml.Data;
using Windows.UI.Xaml.Input;
using Windows.UI.Xaml.Media;
using Windows.UI.Xaml.Navigation;
using Windows.Services.Maps;
using Windows.Devices.Geolocation;
using Windows.UI.Xaml.Controls.Maps;

...
```

```
private async void coffeeButton_Click(object sender, RoutedEventArgs e)
{
    string addressToGeocode = "Red Rock Coffee, Mountain View, CA 94041";

    MapLocationFinderResult result =
        await MapLocationFinder.FindLocationsAsync(
            addressToGeocode, map.Center, 3);

    if (result.Status == MapLocationFinderStatus.Success)
    {
        map.MapElements.Clear();

        foreach(MapLocation location in result.Locations)
        {
            MapIcon icon = new MapIcon();
            icon.Location = location.Point;
            icon.CollisionBehaviorDesired = MapElementCollisionBehavior.RemainVisible;
            icon.Title = "Red Rock Coffee";
            map.MapElements.Add(icon);
        }

        if (result.Locations.Count > 0)
        {
            await map.TrySetSceneAsync(
                MapScene.CreateFromLocationAndRadius(
                    result.Locations[0].Point, 5, 0, 45));
        }
    }
}
```

The button handler begins by defining a string that contains the street address of Red Rock Coffee in Mountain View, California. We pass this address to the MapLocationFinder's FindLocationsAsync method, which takes an address to locate along with a hint point for the location and the number of responses to return. This method is very flexible, and can search for a location by name or can geocode an address.

Once the async method returns, we check for success. Assuming the request succeeded (which it should, unless there's a network problem), we clear any items in the map's MapElements collection, removing any prior MapIcon instances that may be there from a prior search. After that, we create a new MapIcon for each location in the returned result (there should be only one!), setting its location to the search results location, and the title to "Red Rock Coffee." Once we do that, we use the map control's TrySetSceneAsync to position the camera five meters above the terrain with a tilt angle of 45 degrees. Figure 8-2 shows the result.

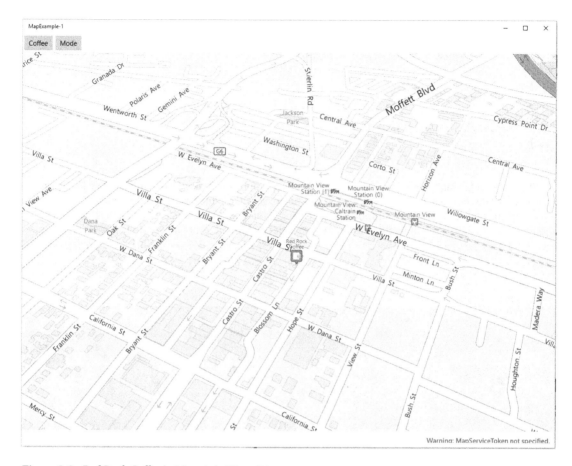

Figure 8-2. *Red Rock Coffee in Mountain View, CA*

Switching Map Modes

This is a nice map and all, but it's kind of dull. Let's switch to an aerial view. Add another button to the button bar in your XAML:

```
<Button x:Name="modeButton" Content="Mode" Margin="3" Click="modeButton_Click"/>
```

Then add Listing 8-4 to the code-behind.

Listing 8-4. Switching map styles

```
private void modeButton_Click(object sender, RoutedEventArgs e)
{
    if (map.Style == MapStyle.Road)
    {
        if (map.Is3DSupported)
        {
            map.Style = MapStyle.Aerial3DWithRoads;
        }
```

```
        else
        {
            map.Style = MapStyle.AerialWithRoads;
        }
    }
    else
    {
        map.Style = MapStyle.Road;
    }
}
```

Note that in Listing 8-4 we check to see if 3D mode is supported before just pushing the style change. That's important, because if we don't do that, on some devices like Windows 10 phones you just won't see a map after switching to an unsupported mode. Once you make this change, you can toggle between aerial and road mode by pushing the button. Aerial mode looks much more interesting, as you can see in Figure 8-3.

Figure 8-3. *Aerial 3D mode over Mountain View, CA*

■ **Tip** When using Aerial 3D mode, consider creating custom XAML for your map icons so they're legible over the varied background terrain.

Showing Streetside Imagery

Finally, let's show the Streetside imagery around Red Rock Coffee. Streetside imagery is especially helpful to users wanting to see an actual location; as we write this, Microsoft has captured imagery for over half the territory by the population of the United States on all public roads, with panoramas taken every few meters.

The same map control can show both maps and Streetside panoramas; you simply pass a custom experience to the control that knows how to render the Streetside data. Let's wire up the map elements so that when you click an icon on the map, the map control shows the Streetside imagery at that location.

To begin, add a click handler to the map in the MainPage constructor, like this:

```
public MainPage()
{
    this.InitializeComponent();
    map.MapElementClick += map_MapElementClick;
}
```

Now, add the click handler in Listing 8-5 to the code-behind.

Listing 8-5. Showing a Streetside panorama when an icon is clicked

```
private async void map_MapElementClick(MapControl sender, MapElementClickEventArgs args)
{
    if (args.MapElements.Count > 0 && args.MapElements[0] is MapIcon)
    {
        MapIcon icon = (MapIcon)args.MapElements[0];

        StreetsidePanorama panorama =
            await StreetsidePanorama.FindNearbyAsync(icon.Location);
        if (panorama != null && map.IsStreetsideSupported)
        {
            map.CustomExperience = new StreetsideExperience(panorama);
        }
        else
        {
            // Indicate whether the panorama wasn't found,
            // or whether Streetside isn't supported.
        }
    }
}
```

This code checks the elements selected to see if the first element is a MapIcon and, if it is, uses the StreetsidePanorama class to find a panorama near the location of the first clicked icon. Assuming there is a panorama near that location, it sets the map's custom experience to a StreetsideExperience and displays the panorama found by the StreetsidePanorama class. Figure 8-4 shows the results. Note that you can zoom and pan in the Streetside panorama, just as you'd expect. If you want a static, non-interactive panorama—a snapshot—you can set the IsEnabled property to false.

Figure 8-4. The Streetside view

Extra Credit: Finding Yourself on the Map

While the map control itself doesn't have an API for geolocation, there is a sensor API in Windows 10 that can use WiFi geolocating or other services to obtain your location. Any Windows 10 Universal application can access this API, as long as the API has "Location" enabled in the package manifest.

Windows 10 provides the Geolocator class in the Windows.Devices.Geolocation namespace. Using it is simple—you create an instance of Geolocator, attach event handlers to its PositionChanged and StatusChanged events, and you're all set. When you create one, the system prompts you whether it's okay for the application to use the device's position; if you click "OK" to answer in the affirmative, the Geolocator instance performs a positioning operation and begins reporting your position through the PositionChanged event. If you decline the request, the Geolocator instance remains in an inactive state, and your handler receives no PositionChanged events.

One wrinkle in all of this is that the sensor system runs on a different thread than the UI thread does, so the actual process of reporting your position involves a cross-thread dispatch from the PositionChanged event handler to your UI thread.

To make this all work in our sample application, we first select Package.appxmanifest in the solution (double-click), and choose "Capabilities" (the third tab in the view that appears). Make sure that "Location" is checked, as you see in Figure 8-5.

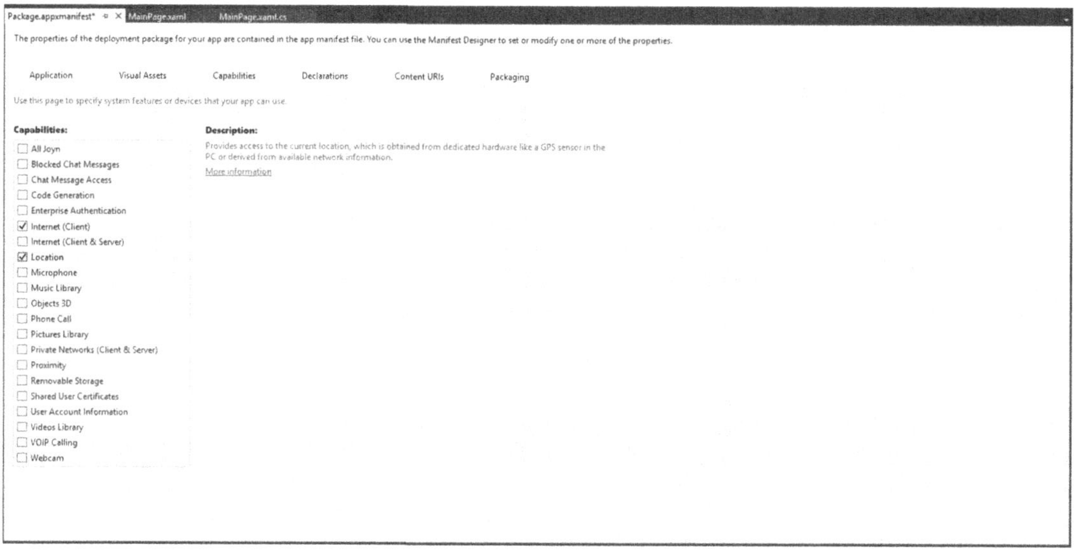

Figure 8-5. Enabling location services in the application manifest

Now, add to MainPage.xaml.cs using directives for the Windows.Devices.Geolocation and Windows. UI.Core. Next, edit the code-behind so that it has the fields and methods you see in Listing 8-6.

Listing 8-6. Enabling positioning in your sample application

```
MapIcon youAreHerePin;
Geolocator geolocator;

public MainPage()
{
    this.InitializeComponent();
    map.MapElementClick += map_MapElementClick;
    Loaded += MainPage_Loaded;
}

private async void map_MapElementClick(MapControl sender, MapElementClickEventArgs args)
{
    if (args.MapElements.Count > 0 &&
        args.MapElements[0] is MapIcon)
    {
        MapIcon icon = (MapIcon)args.MapElements[0];

        StreetsidePanorama panorama =
            await StreetsidePanorama.FindNearbyAsync(icon.Location);
        if (panorama != null && map.IsStreetsideSupported)
        {
            map.CustomExperience = new
                StreetsideExperience(panorama);
        }
        else
```

```
        {
            // Indicate whether the panorama wasn't found,
            // or whether Streetside isn't supported.
        }
    }
}

private void MainPage_Loaded(object sender, RoutedEventArgs e)
{
    geolocator = new Geolocator();
    geolocator.PositionChanged += Geolocator_PositionChanged;
    geolocator.StatusChanged += Geolocator_StatusChanged;
}

private void Geolocator_StatusChanged(Geolocator g, StatusChangedEventArgs e)
{
}

private async void Geolocator_PositionChanged(Geolocator g,
                                    PositionChangedEventArgs e)
{
    await this.Dispatcher.RunAsync(Windows.UI.Core.CoreDispatcherPriority.Normal, () =>
    {
        if (youAreHerePin == null)
        {
            youAreHerePin = new MapIcon();
            map.MapElements.Add(youAreHerePin);
        }
        Geoposition location = e.Position;
        BasicGeoposition position = new BasicGeoposition();
        position.Latitude = location.Coordinate.Latitude;
        position.Longitude = location.Coordinate.Longitude;
        position.Altitude = location.Coordinate.Altitude ?? 0;

        youAreHerePin.Location = new Geopoint(position);
        youAreHerePin.Title = "You Are Here";
    });
}
```

First, we add an event handler for the page's Loaded event, so that we only prompt the user to use location once the application UI has been fully loaded. If we instantiate a Geolocator in the page's constructor, we run the risk of showing the confirmation before the rest of the UI has drawn, which looks bad.

The event handler for the page's Loaded event creates a Geolocator instance and sets up its event handlers. Strictly speaking, we don't need a StatusChanged event handler; you can put a breakpoint there and see the state of the Geocoder change as you accept or deny the location privilege when you're prompted.

The Geolocator_PositionChanged method is an async method that uses await here to signal that the dispatcher's RunAsync method will perform its code on the UI thread, and will not block this thread while that code is running. The dispatcher's RunAsync method takes a priority for the code to run and a lambda expression indicating the code to run.

Our lambda is simple—it lazily constructs a standard MapIcon instance if we don't already have one, and then places the MapIcon at the location reported by the Geolocator. Now, when the application starts, the base map shows a pin with the current location of the device!

Integrating with the Built-In Map Application

The map control is all well and good, but sometimes you want to show some map data without a whole native mapping experience. The Windows 10 Map application registers a URI scheme with Windows that lets you start it to show a map, landmark on a map, query for locations, or request a route between two points.

To do this, you construct a URI with the protocol `bingmaps` and include arguments describing the map you'd like to see. You pass this URI to `Windows.System.Launcher.LaunchUriAsync`, which, as its name indicates, is an `async` method, so your app will probably want to await the results.

Arguments can include:

- the `cp` argument, indicating a latitude and longitude center point (separated by a ~ character);

- the `bb` argument, indicating a bounding box with the coordinates formatted as a south latitude, an underscore, a west longitude, a ~, a north latitude, another underscore, and an east longitude;

- the `where` argument, which is followed by a URIencoded address to geocode;

- the `q` argument, which is followed by a URIencoded string to query Bing for places and show all of the found places in the application;

- the `sty` argument, which can be one of a for aerial, r for roads, or 3d for aerial 3D;

- the `rad` argument, indicating a circular radius for the view in meters;

- the `ss` argument, indicating that the application should open the nearest Streetside panorama to the position passed; and

- the `rtp` argument, consisting of a ~ delimited list of waypoints from which to construct a navigable route.

Here are some sample URIs from the documentation Microsoft provides at `http://bit.ly/1MWIk1j`:

```
bingmaps:?cp=40.726966~-74.006076 /* Opens the Maps app centered over New York City */
bingmaps:?cp=40.726966~-74.006076&lvl=10&q=coffee /* Opens the Maps app and searches for
coffee around that location; sets zoom level 10 to show results */
bingmaps:?where=1600%20Pennsylvania%20Ave,%20Washington,%20DC
bingmaps:?q=coffee&where=Mountain~View, CA /* Opens the Maps app and searches for coffee
near Mountain View, CA */
bingmaps:?rtp=adr.Mountain%20View,%20CA~adr.San%20Francisco%20International%20Airport,%20CA
/* Opens the Maps app with driving directions from a city to a landmark */
bingmaps://?cp=47.6204~-122.3491&ss=1 /*Opens the Maps app with a street-level view of the
Space Needle.*/
```

Wrapping Up

In this chapter, you've seen how to use the Windows 10 map control to display map data in a Windows Universal application, including aerial and Streetside data. You've also seen how you can take control of the built-in Windows 10 Map application to integrate its viewing capabilities in your applications, giving you a lightweight way to display map data.

CHAPTER 9

■ ■ ■

Using Bing Maps REST Services

In addition to the high-level components for building geospatially-aware applications we've described throughout this book, Microsoft provides lower-level building blocks for a lot of their services as representational state transfer (REST) services. Using the Bing Maps REST services, you can

- fetch the latitude and longitude for an address (geocode an address);
- determine the closest address to a latitude or longitude (reverse-geocode a point);
- determine the elevation at a point or get a list of elevations in a region;
- obtain a static image of a map rendered with an optional route or push pins;
- obtain a list of traffic incidents; and
- obtain a human-readable route with walking, driving, or transit directions between two points.

In this chapter, we will first introduce the Bing Maps REST service and then provide the URLs for and a summary of how to use each of these APIs.

Introducing Bing Maps REST Services

Representational state transfer, commonly abbreviated REST, is a common way to encapsulate the client-server interaction required to query and update documents on the web. In REST, URLs provide the nouns describing what information the client application is seeking or updating, and the HTTP protocol verbs such as GET, POST, PUT, and DELETE specify the actions to take on those objects. The data payload between client and server is communicated through the HTTP object body, and client and server both encode the payload using eXtensible Markup Language (XML) or JavaScript Object Notation (JSON).

By providing a REST service for common functions associated with geospatial applications, Microsoft enables you to build applications that transcend the Windows platform. Because REST runs over the Internet using a standard protocol and encoding, you can craft an application for any platform that has an implementation of HTTP and either JSON or XML parsing.

Making the Request

Using the service is easy: you construct a URL that describes the kind of data you want and submit it to the Bing Maps server as an HTTP GET request. (GET is used for all Bing Maps REST Services because you're fetching data from the remote server, rather than updating the content hosted by the server.) As part of the request, you'll indicate whether you want the results as JSON or XML (the default is JSON), and then you will parse the results that come back in the HTTP object body.

As with other Bing Maps APIs, you'll need an API key to access these APIs. An API key comes with a set of usage limits, typically cutting you off if you make more than a set number of requests per hour or per billing period. Go to the Bing Maps Developer Portal at `http://bit.ly/ZmFU3q` and get a key, if you haven't already, or check the API terms and conditions for the key you're using before you deploy your application. You'll include the API key in each of your requests in the URL. For example, if you're geocoding an address in Sunnyvale, your URL might look like this:

```
http://dev.virtualearth.net/REST/v1/Locations?countryRegion=United+States+of+America&
postalCode=94089&addressLine=1020+Enterprise+Way&maxResults=25&key=your-api-key-here
```

Let's look at this request in a little more detail before we get into the specific semantics of the Bing Locations API. You'll note that after the hostname comes the acronym `REST` and a version number, in this case, `v1`. This is common to all Bing Maps REST Service APIs; as we write this, they're all version one. Finally, before the URL-encoded arguments, you'll see the noun, `Locations`. As we previously mentioned, URLs are always nouns in REST; in this specific case, the kind of thing we're interested in is a location, so we pass the noun `Location` in the URL as the ultimate endpoint of the URL. The noun will be different for the different APIs; for example, you pass `Routes/Driving` for driving directions, `Traffic/Incidents` for traffic incidents, and so on. Finally come the arguments for the request; in this case, we're passing a country, a postal code, an address, a cap on the number of results we want returned, and our API key. Of course, these are URLs, so each argument must be URL-encoded; that means + signs for spaces and % escapes for special characters and punctuation. In C#, you can URL-encode strings by invoking the helper function `System.Uri.EscapeUriString`, passing it the string you want to URL-encode. (In ASP.NET, the function `Server.UrlEncode` does the same thing.) The arguments you pass will depend on the REST endpoint you're using, but one thing you'll always need to pass is the key argument, setting it to be equal to your Bing Maps API key. You can also pass the parameter `output` and set it to `xml` to obtain XML responses.

There are a few kinds of argument so common to APIs that they're worth calling out before we get into the specifics of each API. If you need to pass a point on the Earth, you'll pass a latitude and longitude in degrees, separated by a comma. Don't forget that north latitudes are positive, south latitudes are negative, and that west longitudes are negative, while east longitudes are positive; for example, 37.4040,-122.0348 is in Sunnyvale, California, very much *west* of the prime meridian.

You may also need to pass a bounding box, representing a rectangular area on the Earth. You'll pass this as a list of ordinates: first the south latitude, then the west longitude, then the north latitude, then the east longitude. (Think southwest-corner, northeast-corner, and you'll do fine!)

Finally, you can pass an address to many of these APIs, which the API will geocode behind the scenes for you. An address consists of the following:

- The `addressLine` argument, indicating an address relative to the area, such as 1020 Enterprise Way

- The `locality` argument, indicating the populated place, such as a city (but may be a suburb or neighborhood in certain localities)

- The `neighborhood` argument, specifying the neighborhood for an address (such as College Park)

- The `postalCode` argument, specifying the postal code for the address. In the United States, that's the same as the ZIP code.

- The `countryRegion` argument, indicating the country or region.

- The `countryRegionIso2` argument, indicating the ISO two-letter country code for the country.

- The `adminDistrict` and `adminDistrict2` arguments, specifying more specific and less specific administration districts, if applicable.

- The `landmark` argument, which lets you specify a named landmark associated with an address.

Not all of these fields are required in order to define an address. For example, looking at our geocoding request to the Bing Locations API, we only pass the `countryRegion`, `postalCode`, and `addressLine` arguments, letting the geocoder to figure out that Sunnyvale, California, is in the postal (ZIP) code 94089. In general, you should be as specific as you can be when providing addresses.

Understanding the Result

The result of any Bing Maps REST Service request consists of an envelope that contains information about the success or failure of the request, and possibly an array of results for the request. The envelope can contain the following fields:

- The `authenticationResultCode`, which indicates whether or not the Bing Maps API key that you passed is accepted by the server. You should see the value `ValidCredentials` returned for successful authentication of your key. Other values include `InvalidCredentials`, `CredentialsExpired`, `NotAuthorized`, `NoCredentials`, and `None`.

- The `brandLogoUri`, a URL to a logo you can display with the Bing brand for the data you receive. (Your terms of service that you agreed to when obtaining your API key may require you to show this on any output showing results collected from the Bing Maps REST services.)

- The `statusCode`, an HTTP-style status code indicating the success or failure of your request. Look for 200, indicating success.

- The `statusDescription`, a textual description of the status of the request. This will be `OK` on a successful request.

- The `traceId`, a unique identifier for the request

- The `resourceSets` collection, which contains the resources corresponding to the results returned by the REST request

You'll find the actual results of your REST request as items in the `resourceSets` collection, each with a count of the number of results in the `estimatedTotal` field, and the actual results in the collection named `resources`.

For example, the response to our Bing Locations API request looks something like this (with the actual results of the request elided for brevity):

```
{ authenticationResultCode: 'ValidCredentials',
  brandLogoUri: 'http://dev.virtualearth.net/Branding/logo_powered_by.png',
  copyright: 'Copyright © 2015 Microsoft and its suppliers. All rights reserved. This
  API cannot be accessed and the content and any results may not be used, reproduced or
  transmitted in any manner without express written permission from Microsoft Corporation.',
  resourceSets: [ { estimatedTotal: 1, resources: [Object] } ],
  statusCode: 200,
  statusDescription: 'OK',
  traceId: 'a64aad9231f44309bbb40f56c42803f7|CO30276302|02.00.185.2200|CO3SCH010264907,
  CO3SCH010265206' }
```

The Bing Locations API

The Bing Locations API consists of a single noun, `Locations`, to which you either pass an address as an argument, or a list consisting of `Locations` followed by a point so as to reverse-geocode the point and obtain its address. We've already seen an example of a `Locations` request to geocode an address in the previous section; it looked like this:

```
http://dev.virtualearth.net/REST/v1/Locations?countryRegion=United+States+of+America&
postalCode=94089&addressLine=1020+Enterprise+Way&maxResults=25&key=your-api-key-here
```

Making this request of the geocoder returns the following:

```
{ __type: 'Location:http://schemas.microsoft.com/search/local/ws/rest/v1',
  bbox:
   [ 37.40012898164807,
     -122.04147154050406,
     37.40785441678943,
     -122.02850526613656 ],
  name: '1020 Enterprise Way, Sunnyvale, CA 94089',
  point:
   { type: 'Point',
     coordinates: [ 37.40399169921875, -122.03498840332031 ] },
  address:
   { addressLine: '1020 Enterprise Way',
     adminDistrict: 'CA',
     adminDistrict2: 'Santa Clara Co.',
     countryRegion: 'United States',
     formattedAddress: '1020 Enterprise Way, Sunnyvale, CA 94089',
     locality: 'Sunnyvale',
     postalCode: '94089' },
  confidence: 'High',
  entityType: 'Address',
  geocodePoints:
   [ { type: 'Point',
       coordinates: [Object],
       calculationMethod: 'Parcel',
       usageTypes: [Object] },
     { type: 'Point',
       coordinates: [Object],
       calculationMethod: 'Interpolation',
       usageTypes: [Object] } ],
  matchCodes: [ 'Good' ] }
```

There's a lot of data in the response, so let's break it down field by field as follows:

- The bbox field provides a bounding box for the geocoded address, which typically contains the best-known estimate of the address, drawing from both point and parcel address locations.

- The name field contains a human-readable printable name for the address. This is how you'd probably address a letter to the location, and is typically the same as the formattedAddress field of the address field.

- The point field contains the latitude and longitude of the returned address in its coordinates field. Note that these are passed as a list, rather than as named coordinates.

- The `confidence` (a measure of result quality) of the result, a plain-text description.

- The `entityType` field contains the entity type, which is `Address`.

- The `geocodePoints` returns the actual data supporting the geocode operation, which may be a union of information from point address locations, parcels, or interpolated values.

To reverse-geocode a point, you pass the point as the final noun to the Locations REST API, like this:

```
http://dev.virtualearth.net/REST/v1/Locations/37.40399169921875,-122.03498840332031?key=
your-api-key-here
```

Note the difference: the point you're reverse-geocoding isn't an argument—it's part of the noun. You'll get an `Address` entity back, just as for the geocode request, although it may not have as many arguments. For the reverse-geocode URL in our example, you'll see this:

```
{ __type: 'Location:http://schemas.microsoft.com/search/local/ws/rest/v1',
  bbox:
  [ 37.40012898242932,
    -122.04147153718382,
    37.407854417570675,
    -122.02850526281618 ],
  name: '1006 Enterprise Way, Sunnyvale, CA 94089',
  point: { type: 'Point', coordinates: [ 37.4039917, -122.0349884 ] },
  address:
  { addressLine: '1006 Enterprise Way',
    adminDistrict: 'CA',
    adminDistrict2: 'Santa Clara Co.',
    countryRegion: 'United States',
    formattedAddress: '1006 Enterprise Way, Sunnyvale, CA 94089',
    locality: 'Sunnyvale',
    postalCode: '94089' },
  confidence: 'Medium',
  entityType: 'Address',
  geocodePoints:
  [ { type: 'Point',
      coordinates: [Object],
      calculationMethod: 'Interpolation',
      usageTypes: [Object] } ],
  matchCodes: [ 'Good' ] }
```

The fields are the same as for a forward request. You're probably most interested in the `address` field, which contains the specifics of the reverse-geocoded address, and possibly the `geocodePoints` field, which may indicate the supporting data behind the reverse-geocode operation.

The Bing Elevations API

Using the Bing Elevations API, you can obtain the elevation at a point, along a polyline, or at equally spaced locations on the Earth in a bounding box. To do this, you pass one of the nouns Elevation/List, Elevation/Polyline, or Elevation/Bounds, and then either a list of points or a bounding box. For example, to obtain the elevation at a point, we would request something like:

```
http://dev.virtualearth.net/REST/v1/Elevation/List?points=37.40399169921875,
-122.03498840332031&key=your-api-key-here
```

To obtain a list of elevations in a region, you pass the bounding box and the number of rows and columns, like this:

```
http://dev.virtualearth.net/REST/v1/Elevation/Bounds?bounds=37.4,-122,37.45,-122.05&rows=4&
cols=4&key=your-api-key-here
```

The resource in the result contains a list of elevations in meters above sea level. If you pass a single point, you'll receive a single elevation; otherwise, you'll receive a list of elevations. The first elevation corresponds to the southwest corner, and then elevations sweep first to the east and then scan from south to north.

The Bing Routes API

You first saw the Bing Routes API in Chapter 6, where we used it to plot a route on a map. Using the Bing Routes API, you can obtain a route between any two points, specified as addresses (which are geocoded prior to route computation) or geocoordinates. You can obtain driving, walking, or transit directions, depending on the base URL you pass to the API. The base URL for a Bing Routes API request looks like this:

```
http://dev.virtualearth.net/REST/v1/Routes/travelMode
```

Where travelMode is one of Driving, Walking, or Transit. The arguments to the request can include the following:

- waypoint.n, abbreviated wp.n, which is the position (address or geocoordinate) of a waypoint for the computed route

- avoid: optional; a comma-delimited list of values including highways, tolls, minimizeHighways, and minimizeTolls to indicate preferences of things to avoid along the route.

- distanceBeforeFirstTurn: an optional parameter indicating how far in driving directions the driver should go before making their first turn, specified in meters

- heading: an optional argument indicating the initial heading, in degrees from true north

- optimize: how to optimize the route; one of distance, time, timeWithTraffic, and timeAvoidClosure, indicating whether to optimize for distance, time (the default), time including traffic projections, and time taking into account road closures and traffic

- distanceUnit: one of mi or km, indicating whether distances should be reported in miles or kilometers in the resulting route. The default is kilometers.

- dateTime: required for the transit routing directions; indicates the date and time for which the transit route is desired

- timeType: required for transit routing directions, indicating whether the desired time is for Arrival, Departure, or LastAvailable.

Here's an example route URL for driving directions between Sunnyvale, California, and Santa Cruz, California:

```
http://dev.virtualearth.net/REST/v1/Routes/Driving?wp.0=37.40399169921875,
-122.03498840332031&wp.1=Santa+Cruz,CA,USA&key=your-key-hereq
```

The response may contain more than one resource, with each possible route being a single resource. A single route consists of the following fields:

- The actual start and ending points of the route, in the actualStart and actualEnd fields

- The bounding box of the route, in the bbox field

- An id for the route

- The distance unit reported for the route, in the distanceUnit field

- The duration units reported for the route (typically seconds), in the durationUnit field.

- One or more route legs, as a list of route legs in the routeLegs field

- Projected traffic congestion, a textual field, in the trafficCongestion field

- Whether traffic data was taken into account, in the trafficDataUsed field

- The total travel distance, in the travelDistance field

- The duration of the trip, in the travelDuration field

- The projected duration of the trip including traffic, in the travelDurationTraffic field

The results for our example route look like this:

```
{ __type: 'Route:http://schemas.microsoft.com/search/local/ws/rest/v1',
  bbox: [ 36.974018, -122.06958, 37.406071, -121.956959 ],
  id: 'v66,h983696784,i0,a0,cenUS,dAAAAAAAAAAA1,y0,s1,m1,o1,t4,wCyZTA6sGJ_U1~AqbR1O2hLx
AFAADgAXA9Aj8CO~RW5OZXJwcmlzZSBXYXk1~~~,wRF1JAy4eJ_U1~AqbR1O1xhDIFAADgAQWN-T4AO~U2FudGEgQ3
J1eiwgQOE1~~~,k1',
  distanceUnit: 'Kilometer',
  durationUnit: 'Second',
  routeLegs:
   [ { actualEnd: [Object],
       actualStart: [Object],
       alternateVias: [],
       cost: 0,
       description: 'CA-85 S, CA-17',
       endLocation: [Object],
       itineraryItems: [Object],
```

```
      routeRegion: 'NAv2',
      routeSubLegs: [Object],
      travelDistance: 62.527,
      travelDuration: 2236 } ],
  trafficCongestion: 'Heavy',
  trafficDataUsed: 'None',
  travelDistance: 62.527,
  travelDuration: 2236,
  travelDurationTraffic: 3764 }
```

Each route leg consists of the data required to make one leg of the route. In our example, the first route leg looks like this:

```
{ compassDirection: 'north',
  details: [ [Object] ],
  exit: '',
  iconType: 'Auto',
  instruction:
   { formattedText: null,
     maneuverType: 'DepartStart',
     text: 'Depart Enterprise Way toward 11th Ave' },
  maneuverPoint: { type: 'Point', coordinates: [Object] },
  sideOfStreet: 'Unknown',
  tollZone: '',
  towardsRoadName: '11th Ave',
  transitTerminus: '',
  travelDistance: 0.249,
  travelDuration: 18,
  travelMode: 'Driving' }
```

It has the following fields:

- The compassDirection field indicating the direction to go

- The details field, which has fields indicating the actual compass heading, indices of the path to plot on a map if desired, the type of maneuver, the mode (walking, driving, etc.), the name of the route leg, and the type of conveyance of the route leg

- An exit field, if an exit number is available (such as on a freeway)

- An iconType field with an icon indicating the conveyance type

- An instruction, with fields containing the type of maneuver and a textual instruction for the maneuver

- The maneuverPoint field, indicating the geocoordinate at which the maneuver should take place

- The sideOfStreet field, indicating which side of street should be used (used for transit directions)

- The tollZone field, indicating a toll zone

- The `towardsRoadName` field, indicating the road to head toward

- The `travelDistance` and `travelDuration` fields, indicating the distance to travel on this leg in linear and temporal measure

- The `travelMode` field, indicating the modality of travel such as driving, walking, etc.

The Bing Traffic API

Microsoft sources real-time traffic-incident data from sources all over the world. You can use the Bing Traffic API to obtain real-time traffic reports for a region. The REST endpoint you would invoke includes a bounding box for the area of interest. For example, we might request traffic for the region from 37.0 N, 122.0 W to 38.0 N, 121.0 W using the URL:

```
http://dev.virtualearth.net/REST/v1/Traffic/Incidents/37,-122,38,-121?key=your-api-key-here
```

You can pass a severity argument–a list of numbers from one to four indicating the severity of incidents of interest (by default, all severities are reported). You can also pass a list of type integers indicating the types of traffic incidents that should be reported; a full list of types is listed at `http://bit.ly/1hcjbn3` (by default, all traffic types are reported).

Each traffic incident is reported as a separate resource in the resource set returned by the API. Our request presently indicates four incidents, the first of which is an exit-ramp closure at Farmington Road and Ladd Tract Road:

```
{ __type: 'TrafficIncident:http://schemas.microsoft.com/search/local/ws/rest/v1',
  point: { type: 'Point', coordinates: [ 37.94153, -121.23507 ] },
  description: 'At Farmington Rd/Ladd Tract Rd - Exit ramp closed.',
  end: '/Date(1438473674000)/',
  incidentId: 35457971022271800000,
  lastModified: '/Date(1438455374200)/',
  roadClosed: false,
  severity: 4,
  source: 4,
  start: '/Date(1437454874000)/',
  toPoint: { type: 'Point', coordinates: [ 37.94023, -121.23541 ] },
  type: 5,
  verified: true }
```

Incident data includes the following fields:

- The `point` field, indicating the point at which the traffic incident is located

- The `description` field, containing a plaintext description of the incident

- The `end` field, if the end of the incident is known

- The `incidentId` field, a unique ID for the incident

- The `lastModified` field, indicating the last time the traffic incident was updated

- The `roadClosed` field, indicating whether or not the road is closed

- The `severity` field, indicating the severity of the incident

- The `source` field, a numeric identifier indicating the source of the data

- The `start` field, indicating when the incident was first reported

- The `toPoint` field. The point and toPoint fields indicate a span of coverage for the incident.

- The `type` field, indicating the type of incident. Types are a numeric index into a list; for the full list, see `http://bit.ly/1SRGpuu`

- The `verified` field, indicating whether or not the incident has been verified

The Bing Imagery API

Sometimes, what you really want is a picture. The Bing Imagery API provides just that with static map tiles for any region of the world at zoom levels selected to fit the screen and georegion you choose. Unlike the other parts of the Bing REST Services, the returned payload for the Bing Imagery API is an image encoded as either a GIF, JPEG, or PNG, which you can then display in an image-control or web-browser view as part of your content.

The base URL for the Bing Imagery API is `http://dev.virtualearth.net/REST/v1/Imagery/Map/Road/`; you follow that with the type of imagery you'd like to visualize, the center point of the map, and the zoom level of the map, like this:

```
http://dev.virtualearth.net/REST/v1/Imagery/Map/Road/37.40399169921875,122.03498840332031/
14?key=your-api-key-here
```

Note how the center point and zoom level are part of the noun of the REST request; you're actually requesting the imagery *at* that point. The imagery type may be `Map`, as it is in this example, or can be one of the following:

- `Aerial`: Aerial imagery

- `AerialWithLabels`: Aerial imagery with a road overlay

- `Road`: Roads without additional imagery

- `OrdinanceSurvey`: Ordinance Survey imagery, available in some parts of Great Britain

- `CollinsBart`: Collins Bart imagery, available in some parts of Great Britain

In addition to passing the API key, you can pass other arguments to specify the map size in pixels, as well as to indicate the insertion of optional pushpins on the map. For example, the following URL yields the map shown in Figure 9-1:

```
http://dev.virtualearth.net/REST/v1/Imagery/Map/Road/37.40399169921875,-122.03498840332031/14?
mapsize=400,400&pp=37.40399169921875,-122.03498840332031;;1&key=AjbgrYYALE1S87j3_
vdG95k4E1vDZ6RO31Zm89R6Yu2M2yjjHMOOyXEHFM15jW2C&
```

Figure 9-1. *A sample result from the Bing Imagery API*

Here, we're passing the `mapSize` argument to indicate that we want a map that's 400 pixels on a side, and the pushpin argument `pp` indicating that we want a single pushpin at the indicated location with the default style and the label "1". (As of this writing, there are 112 styles of pushpins, and you can see them and their IDs at `http://bit.ly/1JBxBIG`). You can specify up to 18 pushpins as part of the URL, or specify additional pushpins in an object body that you post to the REST endpoint.

Other arguments to the API are:

- `declutterPins`: either 0 (the default) or 1. When 1, attempts to move pushpins so that they don't overlap.

- `format`: One of `GIF`, `PNG`, or `JPEG`, indicating the desired image format. The default is PNG.

- `mapLayer`: When set to `TrafficFlow`, shows traffic flow data on the map

- `mapSize`: The size in pixels; a comma-separated width and height. The default is 350 pixels on a side.

Wrapping Up

The Bing Maps REST API provides a stateless interface to web services for geocoding, reverse-geocoding, elevations, routes, traffic, and obtaining map imagery from the Bing Maps website. Using these APIs, you can build location-aware applications on any platform, including the web, iOS, and Android by using HTTP to make representational state transfer requests of the API and parsing the results, which may be returned as either XML or JSON to your application.

CHAPTER 10

■ ■ ■

Power Map for Excel

While we enjoy programming, we feel there's something to be said for solving a problem without needing to code; after all, no code means no bugs, right? With Power Map, a plug-in for Microsoft Excel Professional and Office 365 Professional, you can create clear geospatial visualizations of your data right from Excel. In many cases involving data visualization, Power Map eliminates the need for programming altogether, letting you work directly with your data in a spreadsheet and see relationships right on a map. Even as a debugging tool, this can be very helpful—you can take a slice of your data from a database, import it into Excel, visualize it, and draw conclusions without needing to write code to plot data on a map.

In this chapter, we will show you how to download and use Power Map, looking at our earthquake data set right from the USGS website. You will learn how to clean up your data for presentation as charts and time series on a map of the Earth, and how to customize the style of the results to meet your needs.

Introducing Power Map

For years, people have cobbled together mapping visualizations on top of Excel. A common trick was to get latitudes and longitudes of your data and then plot data as scatterplots, with the latitude on the x-axis and longitude on the y-axis, using color to differentiate different kinds of data. Still other strategies involved processing the data as much as possible in Excel and then writing a small viewer application to present just points on a map, or building a larger mapping application and embedding an Excel sheet in the application.

Power Map (formerly known as GeoFlow) from Microsoft turns all of that on its head by providing an extension to Microsoft Office Professional and Microsoft Office 365 Professional that accepts data right from Excel and plots the data on maps. Using Power Map, you can

- map data by latitude and longitude or geocode street-address data;

- plot magnitudes on maps as bar charts, bubbles, or heat maps;

- see how data varies over time through animations;

- perform data aggregation such as sums or means and present the data on a map; and

- create still images and videos to embed in presentations.

Figure 10-1 shows Power Map visualizing some earthquakes from the USGS from the previous week.

Getting Power Map is easy, although the minimum requirements set a fairly high bar. You'll need Excel Professional or Office 365 Professional (the Home and Small Business SKUs don't support Power Map), along with at least 3 GB of disk space, and a gigabyte or two of RAM. As with most data-visualization tasks, the bigger your data set, the more RAM you should have. You also need to ensure that you have DirectX 10 or better, as the mapping visualizations make heavy use of your graphics card. Finally, while using Power Map you need to have an Internet connection, because both the map data and geocoding use Microsoft's servers as a source of data.

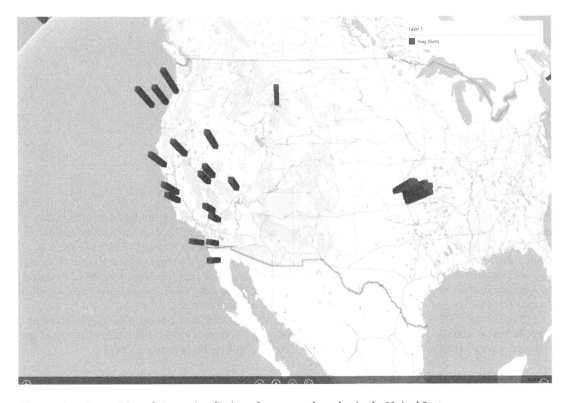

Figure 10-1. *Power Map editing a visualiation of recent earthquakes in the United States*

If you meet these requirements, the Power Map menu item will be visible in Excel's Insert toolbar.

Getting Started with Power Map

The USGS offers earthquake data in a variety of formats, one of which is a comma-separated-value (CSV) file sorted by time. Go to `http://on.doi.gov/1dvKf9X` and pick a file; in the example that follows, we're using the file of earthquakes from the previous seven days, because it's enough data to experiment with without being overwhelming.

The data has a number of fields, but the fields we'll focus on are:

- The time (which we'll need to convert to a time Excel can process for our time-series animation)

- The latitude and longitude of the earthquake event

- The magnitude of the earthquake event

- The depth of the earthqake event

Download a data set from the USGS and save it as an Excel file (you can't directly work with CSV files in Power Map, as the Power Map visualizations are saved as part of the Excel file). Before we begin our visualiation, though, we need to do something about the format of the earthquake times: they are expressed as strings in a standard format, rather than as seconds from the beginning of an epoch for Excel to process. To fix this, let's add a column "converted" in column P with a formula to convert those strings to something more useful:

1. In cell P1, enter a label like converted date. It doesn't matter what you use here, as long as you know what it's for.

2. Select column P, right-click, and choose "Format Cells." Pick Date from the list that appears, and choose the format "3/14/12 13:30."

3. In cell P2, enter the formula as follows:

```
=VALUE(MID(A2,6,2)&"/"&MID(A2,9,2)&"/"&LEFT(A2,4)&"
"&MID(A2,12,2)&":"&MID(A2,15,2)&":"&MID(A2,18,2))
```

4. Copy this formula to the remaining cells of column P that have data.

The formula is simple, but a little difficult to parse out. It takes the month, day, year, hour, minute, and second fields as characters of the string in cell A2, builds a new string in month/day/year hour:minute:second format, and then passes that string to the VALUE function to get the date value for that string. The MID function takes a cell, the starting character to return, and the number of characters to return, while the LEFT function takes a cell and the number of characters on the left to return. The & operator just builds up strings; it's the string concatenation operator in Excel.

You should now be able to start Power Map by choosing Launch Power Map from the Power Map menu on the Insert tab, as you see in Figure 10-2.

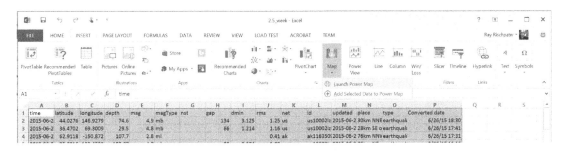

Figure 10-2. *Launching Power Map. Note our augmented data set, with USGS timestamps on the left and the computed Excel timestamps on the right*

Navigating around Power Map

Power Map lets you construct what it calls *tours* of your data—visualizations of the data in time and space. A tour is just a map with some data (possibly data over time) that the user can manipulate; you can construct multiple tours that highlight different aspects of your data.

When you launch Power Map, you'll be asked to add a tour to or open an existing tour in Power Map, and then you will see the main screen (Figure 10-3). It's divided up into the following sections:

- The menu bar across the top, which gives you the basic controls to Power Map.

- The visualizations present in a specific tour, which are in the leftmost column

- A map (either a flat map or a globe of the Earth) in the center column

- The layer and layer-properties editor in the rightmost column

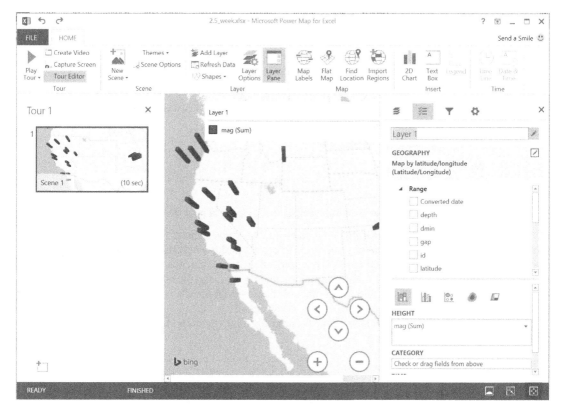

Figure 10-3. *The Power Map main screen, with the views on the left, the view of the map in the center, and the layer editor on the right*

Let's add a plot of the magnitudes of our earthquakes to the tour we're creating.

1. Power Map should recognize the latitude and longitude fields in your data. If it doesn't, in the layer editor, drag them to the bottom "Geography and Map Level" box and mark them `latitude` and `longitude`.

2. Click Next in the layer editor.

3. For Type, choose `Column`.

4. For Height, drag `mag` to the Height box.

You should now see something similar to Figure 10-1, with a timeline below the map of the Earth. Click the Play button to see an animation of the earthquakes in your data set plotted over time.

Map Options in Power Map

Let's take a closer look at the options in Power Map in Figure 10-3. On the menu bar across the top, we have the following buttons:

- Play Tour plays all of the open scenes of a tour, one after the other, with transitions between each tour, in fullscreen. This item is grouped with related items for producing a final visualization of your scene, like Create Video, Capture Screen, and Tour Editor.

- New Scene lets you add a new scene to the tour. Scenes have layers, which we'll describe in more detail in a minute. This includes options for the current scene, as well as a drop-down menu to let you set the theme of the scene.

- Layer Options within the Layer Pane lets you add map layers, refresh the data from the spreadsheet, and draw shapes on the map.

- Map Labels shows and hides the map labels on the map.

- Flat Map toggles between a view of the world as a globe and a flat map using the Mercator projection.

- Find Location has you enter an address (such as a street address, or a more general location such as a city or postal code), and the map will zoom in on that address. It's handy when you're trying to get a handle on how your data relates to a specific location.

- 2D Chart lets you superimpose a bar chart or other graph of the ordinate you're plotting on the map in the scene. You can use it to summarize data that should both be seen spatially and summarized.

- Textbox lets you drop a text box over the map in the scene, where you can add additional information such as a caption to your scene.

- Legend lets you add a legend to your scene, which you should definitely do if your scene includes more than one layer.

- Time Line includes the time controller for time-series data on the map in the scene, so the user can scrub through a timeline, start and stop playback, and so forth.

- Date & Time toggles a label containing the current date and time during time series playback.

Configuring the Presentation of a Layer

Each scene in a tour lets you add one or more layers to the map. A layer is a collection of geocoded data that may vary in time. Layers have a geographic component—either a latitude and longitude or an address to locate the data point on the map in the layer—and one or more bits of data that should be plotted on the map in some way.

When creating a layer, the first thing you do is specify the geography for the layer by indicating the columns of the spreadsheet that should be parsed for position data. If your data is already geocoded, you need only indicate the latitude and longitude fields (one datum per column, please!). If your data is not geocoded, but consists of things such as addresses or city names, never fear: Power Map will geocode data, including partial data such as city and state, or just the state or country, for the position data. Again, you'll just select the columns of data and indicate their type (street or city or state or country), and Power Map does the rest in plotting.

Data for a layer can be rendered in one of four ways:

- Column, which places a bar-graph style display at each geographic position for each data point

- Bubble, which places a bubble sized to the relative size of the data at each geographic position

- HeatMap, which renders redder colors for denser aggregations of data points

- Region, which aggregates data by city, state, zip code, or country and colors regions based on the magnitude of the data in the region

Which one you choose isn't just a matter of choice; column presentation is best for a few discrete points, or for points widely spaced over the Earth. Bubble rendering is less exact than column rendering, and is a good choice when you're trying to distinguish the relative magnitude of things. Heat maps are excellent when you want to see the relative density of something—say, crime statistics or the like. And region plotting needs your data to be binned not by point but by region, so that you can visually compare distinct regions such as states against the statistic you're examining.

The value for a point on your map can be from one column in your spreadsheet, or several. Power Map can aggregate data points into a single statistic in a variety of ways:

- By taking the sum of the statistics

- By taking the average (arithmetic mean) of the statistics

- By taking the count (not blank) or distinct count of the statistics

- By taking the minimum or maximum of the statistics

If you need a more sophisticated analysis of the data (say, is the statistic greater than the three-sigma threshhold of all of your data), don't forget that you have the full power of Excel behind Power Map—just dive into Excel, make a new column, and add a formula that does what you want.

If you're plotting a time series, the time can be binned by day, month, quarter, or year, and you can present points cumulatively, so that previous data points stay on the map as new points are plotted, or only show each data point for an instant. To change this last facet of presentation, click the clock icon to the right of the Time field label, and choose either "Data shows for an instant" "Data accumulates over time," or "Data stays until it's replaced."

Styling the Power Map Result

From the menu bar, you can make gross styling changes to the map using the Themes button, or by choosing a flat map instead of a globe if that's your preferance. Your choices of a map theme include some photorealistic and some symbolic maps, and some stylized maps that are best used for showing rough relationships. These themes also come with some default colors for labels; this is nice if your skills don't lend themselves to graphic design. The text boxes, legend, and the date and time labels you can apply from the legend are all movable, too, so you can position them around key parts of your map and avoid obscuring critical information.

In the task pane, the gear icon for a layer takes you to the layer options and scene options. From the layer option, you can adjust the relative size of data points being plotted (making bars higher or shorter, for example, or bubbles more or less chunky) as well as adjust the color used to plot the data for a layer if it's appropriate (you can't change the color of heat maps or region maps). You can also choose whether Power Map presents zeros or negative data; of course, you could do that with a bit of Excel wizardry in the data, if you'd prefer.

Finally, in the scene options, you can adjust how long a scene is shown (handy if you're plotting time series) and give the scene a name. You can also control the transition from one scene to the next, using a number of transitions provided. All of this is visible when you choose Play Tour from the menu bar, or make a video of your tour for export to the Internet or inclusion in another document.

Wrapping Up

Sometimes, all you need to do is plot your data on a map for a presentation. While you can do this using any of the Bing Maps controls you've learned about in this book, Power Map for Excel is also an option if you have Excel Professional (or Office 365 Professional) and your data fits in a spreadsheet. You can make animated presentations of data rendered as columns, heat maps, bubbles, or by region; you can also aggregate the data and process the data using all of the power of Microsoft Excel.

Index

■ X, Y, Z

Get the eBook for only $5!

Why limit yourself?

Now you can take the weightless companion with you wherever you go and access your content on your PC, phone, tablet, or reader.

Since you've purchased this print book, we're happy to offer you the eBook in all 3 formats for just $5.

Convenient and fully searchable, the PDF version enables you to easily find and copy code—or perform examples by quickly toggling between instructions and applications. The MOBI format is ideal for your Kindle, while the ePUB can be utilized on a variety of mobile devices.

To learn more, go to www.apress.com/companion or contact support@apress.com.

Printed in the United States
By Bookmasters